M000074243

Mʀ ROMANCE'S
BOOK OF
LOVE

MR. ROMANCE'S

BOOK OF LOVE

Passionate Secrets of America's Greatest Lovers

Langdon Hill

KNIGHT-RIDDER
PRESS

©1986 by Langdon Hill

Published by the Knight-Ridder Press
A Division of HPBooks, Inc.
P.O. Box 5367, Tucson, AZ 85703
(602) 888-2150

Printed in U.S.A.
9 8 7 6 5 4 3
First Printing December 1986

Library of Congress Cataloging in Publication Data

Hill, Langdon.
  Mr. Romance's book of love.

    1. Love—Anecdotes, facetiae, satire, etc.
I. Title. II. Title: Mr. Romance's book of love.
III. Title: Book of love
HQ801.A2H54   1986   306.7   86-82239
ISBN: 0-89586-494-0

*To the world's smallest romantic
with the world's largest heart:
Marian Langdon Hill Terry*

Contents

Foreword

Remember when we naively believed that true love lasted forever—before children, money, age and other responsibilities proved us foolish?

Well, *Mr. Romance's Book of Love* proves that we weren't so foolish after all! In the same entertaining way that made *How to Jump-Start Your Husband* so successful, Langdon Hill shows all of us how America's Greatest Lovers keep romance alive, in spite of life's everyday obstacles and crises. These intimate, true-life success stories prove that long-lasting romance is possible for everyone.

You'll laugh and you'll cry. And when you finish this book, you'll turn to that partner of yours with a new light in your eye and renewed love in your heart. It's must reading for anyone who has ever been in love and wants to be in love again.

Parris Afton Bonds
Author of *Blue Bayou*

Introduction:
You Are Undeniably
One of America's
Greatest Lovers

This is a how-to book unlike any other how-to book you've ever read. The advice comes not from psychologists with impressive degrees but from real-life lovers with impressive stories to tell. Through these stories you're going to learn more about finding love, improving love, making love and staying in love. And you're going to have more fun at it than you've ever had before.

But there is a catch. Having spent the past five years writing a nationally syndicated newspaper column on romance, I've grown to distrust two things—neither of which you'll find in this book.

First is any "expert" who claims to know more than you do. Second is an "expert's conclusion," which frequently only proves that these same folks don't know diddly. The *real* experts are America's Greatest Lovers, who have fought in the trenches of passion and who have battled at hand-to-hand romance. The *other* "experts" learned from reading books; our real-life experts write the book of love every day.

Don't get me wrong. I can enjoy listening to the warm and wonderful spoutings of today's pop love psychologists just as much as you do. But these well-meaning folks have lived only their own lives. Each gives advice based on his or her own limited experience. And nowhere do the limits of their experience show through more clearly than when you ask these amorous academicians the tough questions. Questions like:

♥ How can parents enjoy romance with kids jumping into every hug?

♥ How can a single woman find love when everyone says the odds are ten-and-a-half zillion to one?

♥ How can a man get romantic when the last thing he revved up was his Packard . . . four decades ago?

♥ And how, exactly, can a couple add real newness and spontaneity to their sex life after having sweated backwards and forwards through the Kama Sutra?

These are tough questions. So, what do these love psychologists give as their "answers"? They'll tell you to:

♥ "Assert your desires."

- ♥ "Be more sensitive."
- ♥ "Open up your feelings."
- ♥ "Forget old stereotypes."
. . . and the real biggie,
- ♥ "Communicate."

Great. We know that already. We hear it all the time. Why can't they tell us something new? Why can't they be more specific?

I'll tell you why. The only way you can learn the specific, practical, real-world solutions to love is to find them out for yourself—or to learn them from someone who has. And the only people who have done that are America's Greatest Lovers.

"So," I can hear you demanding, "who the heck are America's Greatest Lovers?" Are they guys like the Hollywood studlet whose gluteus maximus has won more campaigns than a Roman rear admiral? Or are they women like the sultry cinema siren whose waterbed has run up more mileage than a 1957 Volvo? No, friend, America's Greatest Lovers are intelligent and caring people. America's Greatest Lovers are people just like you.

Yes, you read right. Take a good look at yourself in a mirror. What do you see? ("A fitness-era soul in a Twinkie-generation body.") Nope, you're staring at a human being with rare intelligence and perception; a human being who knows what he or she wants, but who could use some good ideas on how to get it.

That's exactly what *Mr. Romance's Book of Love* offers. Practical, concrete, ready-to-use ideas and inspiration for making your life even more passionate. I've spent five years collecting these types of stories from great lovers everywhere, and I've selected the best for this book.

And, just for fun, I've even thrown in a little psychology. ("No Langdon, amigo, don't tell us you've already gone over to the other side?") Heck, no. The kind of psychology this book offers belongs to this planet. It comes from real people, and it provides real inspiration.

Say, for example, your lovelife is in a rut. You've gotten a little too routine in your routine and you're experiencing little intimacy in your intimacy. Your romance has run smack dab into an apparently insurmountable obstacle. What do you do? Well, America's Greatest Lovers will tell you.

Stories in Chapter 1 will show you how people like you have triumphed over even the most imposing obstacles. And stories in Chapter 2 tell you *exactly* how lovers have repeatedly created the right romantic atmosphere for spontaneity and surprise.

You want a sample? OK, let's handle problem number one: "My romance has run into the brick wall of life." One of this book's obstacle-busting answers comes from Dennis and Cheryl Shepard. Their inspiring story says worlds more about succeeding against all odds than any globe-trotting psychologist. It is told by their friend, Alamo Reaves, and reads:

Dear Mr. Romance:

I would like to nominate Dennis Shepard as the World's Greatest Lover. Dennis met Cheryl on the University of Arizona campus when their guide dogs lunged at each other. It turned out that the dogs were litter sisters who had been raised and trained at Guide Dogs for the Blind in San Raphael, California.

Although Dennis, blind from birth, and Cheryl, blinded as a young adult from a rare disease, went through different training sessions when they got their dogs and consequently never met, the dogs recognized each other and brought them together here in Tucson.

Their courtship was complicated by Dennis's schooling, Cheryl's need for a kidney transplant, and the side effect of drugs she took to try and save her eyesight. But Dennis was finally able to pop the question on New Year's Day 1984, and he made sure they were on cloud nine at the time by taking her up in a hot-air balloon to ask her to marry him.

At the wedding, Dennis, a member of a barbershop quartet, sang "Heart of My Heart," as Cheryl walked down the aisle on her father's arm. The dogs were also in the wedding procession, with flowers braided on their harnesses. And a nurse from the dialysis treatment center, where Cheryl had spent long hours before her transplant, also sang.

Because of Cheryl's health problems, no one is sure

how long the romance will last and, in fact, it almost ended last winter when Cheryl contracted a severe infection and had difficulty fighting it because of the immuno-suppressive drugs. Her parents would stay with her at the hospital by day while Dennis was at work, and he would stay with her all evening, often after the buses stopped running, and would be led home by his dog— on foot—over three miles to their apartment across town.

But Dennis doesn't brood about the things that could happen tomorrow. He makes today happy for Cheryl with an endless stream of jokes, poems, gifts, songs he writes for her and things to make her laugh and love. He won't ever see his bride, but Dennis Shepard's vision of the real meaning of love is greater than anyone else's I know. ♡

The real meaning of love. If you want to find it, ask the real experts. Ask just a few of the lovers who tell their passionate secrets and stories in this book:

Sally and Clayton Young, who found love late in life and are determined to let nothing stop them from keeping it "forever."

P. T. Thompson, who discovered the key to her lover's heart (and other valuable parts) on "The Night Modesty Blazed."

The Pence Family, who found their secret to love and the baby boomlet.

Patrick, an observant fourth-grader, who tells all parents to go ahead and get romantic when he reveals: "I know my parents love each other because every time my Dad comes home, he always gets my Mom from behind, puts his hands around her waist, picks her up, takes her back into the bedroom. Next thing I know the shower's running."

Linda Carlson, who learned the meaning of spousal patience and understanding when she fell asleep in her husband's "cuddling" arms after working an all-night shift.

Lorne Greene, who shows us that—even for super-stars—the fondest memories are frequently created by the smallest moments.

Eric Kingsford, who captured his lover's heart by fulfilling her strangest fantasy.

Carole Johnson, who dared to believe in her wildest dreams.

Debbie Kirby, who can only smile when her kids say, "Aw Mom, aw Dad, not AGAIN! Kissie, kissie, kissie."

These are America's real romance experts—and so are you. You know what you like, you know what you need, and you know what's right for you. And this book will show you how to get it.

OK, so that's a lot, but remember the catch. These are not "answers" in the traditional sense. These are stories of how real-life lovers have very successfully handled specific real-life problems. In short, America's Greatest Lovers have put together the most inspirational operator's manual ever known. The hands-on romance application is up to you.

Love Knows No Obstacles, No Barriers and Has (Thankfully) Damn Little Common Sense

After watching an evening of American TV, you're bound to wonder if love makes sense anymore. I mean, really, what can you say about a culture that's picked Joan Collins as its embodiment of refinement and romance? Damn little if you ask me.

It's not that I've got anything personal against Joan. Really. If I were looking for an actress to star in "Lovestyles of the Rich and Raunchy," Alexis would be my first choice. But I just don't think the fabled Joan of Arching knows the first thing about "romance."

"So Langdon," I can hear you asking, "Tell us, what *is* romance?"

Good question. Romance is everything you do to show someone you care. Let's try that again—Romance is everything (and anything) you do to show someone (anyone) you care. It's that note you snuggled next to your hubby's tuna-salad sandwich. It's that pen holder you made for your mom in first grade. It's that defrosting hug you gave to your partner in front of the frozen peas at the supermarket. Yes, even today, romance is alive.

Now, I can hear the screams of much-too-macho slimeballs from coast to coast: "Romance is alive! Secure the doors, cover the ceiling mirrors, stash the industrial-strength musk in the safe! It's alive!"

Pardon this outburst, but you see, in the past few years a lot of people have been trying to kill romance. For example, in the late 1970's it was:

Mucho Macho Men such as Erik Estrada in the TV show *C.H.I.P.S.* This hunk made money saying things like, "Hey baby, whadya' say we glide on my Suzuki tonight?" These macho-do-about-nothing guys were the only human beings in the world who shopped at Sears for party packs of Pennzoil.

But after the rise and fall of these guys you had to watch out for:

Mega-Mellow Males as typified by Alan Alda. Sure they are truly great guys, but they are just *so* sensitive and *so* sincere that such men would ask their dates, "Darling, I know we haven't even saved a single whale yet, but it's been three months. Do you think it would deeply violate your Id if I kissed you?" You've heard of the strong, silent type. These guys were too often just plain weak and whimpering.

And today in our no-holds-barred world of romance, you have to keep from being body-slammed by:

Prime-Time Passion Poppers. If you spend an evening a week in "Dallas" and regularly brush with "Falcon Crest," then you know that prime-time romance takes little more than a look, a leap and a lap.

So who the heck knows the most about romance? Obviously not these folks. (And don't look at me. In the true tradition of a reporter, I collect *your* stories and ideas. The imposing title "Mr. Romance" was the product of an overzealous headline writer.) The true Mr. and Ms. Romance of the world are *you.* Through your letters, phone calls and interviews, I've learned many secrets of romance. And the first is (drumroll) that *love knows no obstacles, no barriers and has (thankfully) damn little common sense.*

If there is one misconception about romance, it's that it takes the right moment, the right ambience and the right underarm deodorant to make it work. Dear reader, it takes none of the above. None. El zippo.

Good, loving, fun-filled romance can happen no matter what kind of shlock is thrown at it. Remember the blind couple who met when their guide dogs lunged at each other?

Well, they're not alone in the Love-Despite-All-Odds category. While most of us are complaining about

11

the lack of good movies on HBO, there are millions of people surviving and succeeding through *real* challenges. For many of these Great American Lovers, the only thing they haven't lost is their belief in love. But they've discovered that their belief—their inspiration—is worth everything.

Obviously, then, the first $64,000 question is "Where did these couples find their inspiration?" And the second prize-winning query is "How do couples in love discover the wisdom to overcome obstacles?"

Let's start with the latter. There's a truism that says, "No human can find true wisdom until he or she has experienced poverty, love and war." Therefore, to answer the second question, many couples find all three keys to wisdom soon after they find each other. But they don't learn how to use those keys most effectively until they are blessed by, you guessed it, inspiration. And you'd be surprised where that comes from.

For example, a woman named Sally Young found her inspiration in beautiful silk scarves and sexy tan legs. A lover named Louise Evans discovered her will to go on through her husband's indefatigable sense of humor. And a romantic named Sally Davis found her vision of love in a perfect picture window.

So who in heaven are these people? They're the authors of just a few of the inspiring stories you're about to read. And what is their message? Put simply, it's:

"If we can solve our problems, or overcome any obstacle, or find our inspiration, so can you."

A word of warning before you go on, though. This is powerful stuff. These are real stories of the real heroes of romance. They don't pull any punches. They tell, blow by blow, of their bouts with poverty, illness, handicaps and death. While each story has a happy ending, each has a far-from-joyous beginning.

So here's some advice: I suggest that you read just one or two of the stories in this chapter and then take a break. The key word here is "inspiration." Read until you feel inspired—and I promise that you will—and then go to the next chapter. After a few laughs there, you may want to come back to read a couple more stories here. Treat the remaining stories as "islands of encouragement" to be used later on.

The following Great American Lover lives in Seattle with her husband. She was inspired enough to submit this extraordinary tale called:

THE LOVE STORY OF
CLAYTON & SALLY YOUNG (FOREVER)
by Mrs. Sally Young

Talk about romance! Clayton and I happily have it in all aspects, in the fullest sense of the word, and I have just never been able to keep my mouth shut about it. After being married for almost four years now, Clayton has adjusted to this enthusiasm of mine and enjoys it and adds to it. You see, when two people find the love and romance of their lives later on in life (I am in my early 50's and Clayton is in his early 60's), it takes you by surprise, and you just can't take such love for granted.

Why am I so crazy about Clayton? He has an intelligent mind that I respect; he is spiritually beautiful; he has the utmost integrity; he has a very distinguished demeanor and handsome looks; he has a wonderful sense of humor and makes me laugh often; and last, but not least, he has a great body.

Clayton's feelings about me are reflected in the way he is always taking me out on romantic dates and giving me things to look forward to, especially on Friday "Fun Nite" when we go dancing. He also cares about the color and style of my clothes and helps me select everything from clothes, to jewelry, to color of makeup, and he buys me lots of surprises. He says that as an architect he enjoys beauty in all its forms and he is definitely turned on by me and that in turn, turns me on. I know this sounds personal, but how wonderful that this can be true at any age.

Up until four months ago, my letter would have stopped here. Since then a new dimension has been added to our lives where our love and romance have encountered new and unexpected parameters. Four months ago we were told that I have a very rare and deadly form of cancer called angio sarcoma. This aggressive cancer is carried through the bloodstream and forms tumors throughout the body—of which I

have a macroscopic one so far in my breast. So many
things in our lives have changed now, but not our love
and—Yes—romance, too. Clayton says that this has
given us an even greater and deeper meaning to an
already superb relationship. We both feel it.

Here I am now with no hair, a Hickman catheter
hooked up to my heart and a long tube exiting from my
left breast, soon to have a mastectomy on my right
breast, receiving chemotherapy in the hospital 6 days
out of every 28, a prognosis that this is only the beginning if I am lucky, only a short period each month when
the effects from chemotherapy are reasonable—and yet
my husband treats me like I am beautiful and still makes
dates with me and gives me things to look forward to.

If you were to see us you would not feel sorry for us, as
who of us is given a guarantee in life? What you would
feel instead is joy for us, as we have such a love to
share—and believe me, even now, it is not just a love of
companionship, etc. I get all dressed up "fit to kill" the
way my husband finds attractive and we go out to dinner
and we go dancing, to art openings, symphony, etc. and
enjoy the companionship of friends and Clayton makes
a big deal out of it to give me something exciting to look
forward to.

For my bald head (wigs are uncomfortable and
scratchy), he took me to Nordstrom's and selected some
very beautiful silk scarves, hats and earrings to go with
them. He makes me feel like a model when I wear them.
We will be concentrating on sexy tan legs this summer

instead of low cut blouses. We have less quantity of good times, but more quality.

This letter has come directly from my heart to this typewriter and though this may end up being a jumble of wonderful feelings about my husband and me, it is something I felt I had to do and say.

Yes, we have ROMANCE in our marriage and when it is true and respectful and deep, it will always be there no matter what challenges are ahead. We are proof. ♡

I told you this was powerful stuff.

By the way, thanks to KING-TV in Seattle I was able to talk to Sally and Clayton in person after I received their letter. Sally told me that the Friday after her mastectomy—three days after her surgery—she and Clayton went out dancing. I asked her, "You had surgery on Tuesday and then went dancing three nights later?" And Sally smiled at me, touched my arm lightly and said, "Of course, Langdon. Friday is our 'Fun Nite.'"

Sally and Clayton are certainly not alone in their fight for real fun and real romance. Their belief in the healing power of love is shared by thousands of Americans. Americans like Mrs. Louise Evans, who is married to:

AMERICA'S GREATEST
HUSBAND, FATHER & LOVER
by Mrs. Louise Evans

My husband, Jack, and I will be married 24 years this

16

November. This, in itself, takes a great amount of love. However, I consider Jack to be America's Greatest Lover because he encouraged me to go to the university when our children were small so that I could obtain my lifetime dream, a degree from the college of nursing.

OK, so you might say "Big deal." Believe me, it was. This was no easy task since we had one hyperactive child who had asthma and suffered seizures while our other child had been diagnosed as having brain damage. It would be an understatement to say both children required a great deal of our time.

My husband, this marvelous man, four years prior to my attending the university, had been diagnosed as having a rare type of muscular dystrophy. Some men might just be deep in self-pity with their own problem when told they had an incurable disease, let alone handle that and all our additional family problems. But not *my* husband. He lovingly took care of the children, sent me to college, helped me with my studies, constantly encouraged me and completely took over my role at home. He continued to keep his marvelous sense of humor in spite of the many nights he spent without sleep when a child was sick and he would insist I sleep.

Jack may not always bring me flowers, but his great bouquet is a love that has kept our family strong. Now, he has seen his son and daughter grow to maturity— encouraging them every step of the way, loving them and teaching them (and me) more about unselfish love than any one human could teach another. Now, if he knew I wrote this letter he'd probably say that he wasn't special, but I know he is. And I am so very proud to be, Mrs. Jack Leroy Evans. ♡

(Mr. Romance Note: Now that you've experienced some heavy-duty heart-warming, this would be a great time to jump ahead to the body-warming suggestions in Chapter 2, starting on page 27. Don't worry. The rest of the stories will be right here to inspire you when you come back.)

Also proud to be in love is a woman known to her husband as:

AMERICA'S MOST BEAUTIFUL WOMAN
by Mrs. Cathleen Perez

I wish to submit my husband, Joseph A. Perez, as America's Greatest Lover. Joseph and I have been married for five years. From the beginning, he "swept me off my feet." Our first date lasted 29 hours. In the third hour he proposed. To my great surprise, then and now, I accepted.

Six months into our marriage, while living in Wyoming, the cold weather literally crippled me with arthritis. Joseph had to carry me to the bathroom, wash my hair, cook, keep house *and* work to support us. One day, as he carried me in from my bath, I started crying. I sobbed, "It's not fair. We've only been married six months and you're stuck with a cripple."

I'll never forget what he said: "You shut up. I'm getting to take care of the most beautiful woman in the world. I've got no complaints." Truly, I am very lucky and very blessed. ♡

I've got no complaints. That's one of the key ingredients to the mystery of love. These true American heroes look for the good—and the love—in all things. Cynics might say that people in love have damn little common sense. Thank God for that. It's these lovers' uncommon sense that makes our wart-filled world a less bumpy and more beautiful place. And it's that same uncommon sense that helped a beautiful woman named Sally Davis deal smoothly with the most difficult of times. Her story is called:

A WINDOW OF LOVE ON THE WORLD
by Mrs. Sally Davis

As a nominee for America's Greatest Lover, I really feel that my husband Richard is qualified. His unique way of showing his affection at this point includes totally caring for me as a terminal cancer patient.

Dick does all the laundry, shopping, cooking, and cleaning and holds down a full-time construction job while maintaining 22 rental units all over town. He also helps my parents (who are 75 years old) with anything they need.

Every time he comes home he has a special treat for

me, whether it be something to tempt my appetite, flowers, plants or a small gift. Every time Dick leaves, he always tells me where he'll be, when he'll be back and never forgets an "I love you" sealed with a kiss.

After we found out that I have only months to live, he designed and constructed an addition to our house. My bedroom/den with closet and bathroom overlooks "my" beautiful mountains, which give me total peace and serenity. The area includes two large sliding glass doors through which I can view the birds eating from the bird feeders he put up. For my enjoyment, he also added a fireplace and sliding mirrored doors for the closet and bathroom, which reflect the lights of the foothills at night.

This was Dick's contribution to the process of our accepting our final separation. I wasn't able to help with the choices and decisions of building my room, and yet it was built absolutely the way I would have wanted it had I been able to help.

Considering we've been married only two years and he married me one week after my first cancer surgery, it seems to me that Dick has a better understanding of what love, caring, sharing and marriage are all about than should be humanly possible. ♡

Sally's letter was hand-delivered by her daughter. She wanted me—and the world—to read it as a loving testimonial. Sally Davis died soon after it was written. But not one of these true American heroes wants you to feel sorry for them. If anything, they want us to know that our all-too-brief lives can be the source of everlasting love. As they have said, their problems have simply been put into "proper perspective." And for some great lovers that perspective comes at a tender age.

Take Greg Kelly, for example. He wrote the following letter just to tell me of his love for his family. I've left Greg's spelling, and feelings, intact:

I LOVE MY MOTHER & FATHER
by Greg Kelly

Our mom got sick back in August. Dad has been doing The laundry, shopping and cooking. He gets up for work at 4:30 of a morning and don't go to bed late at night.

Me and my brothers (David and Leslie) Help by cleaning the house and washing dishes while dad works.

Dad set up a bed for mom so she can get her rest. Dad set a bed in one corner of the room so he can be near her if she needs anything. Just because mom got sick, it didn't change our love for her or dad's love for her.

We Know and pray she will get better. Mom has to go to the hospital 1 more week for radiation treatment and we hope that's all.

P.S. Our mom had a brain tumor operation and is getting better. Sincerly yours,

Greg Kelly, 11 years of age. ♡

As you can see, Greg has had to pack an awful lot of

wisdom into just 11 years. He learned—in heroic form—that nothing stops love. This same lesson, along with a direct lesson on the helping power of romance, is also passionately detailed in the following story called:

IF YOU COULD HEAR WHAT I CAN HEAR
by Billie Marie Studkos

My romantic experience is unusual. Handicapped by 60% hearing loss, deserted by the father of my three pre-schoolers, humiliated as a welfare recipient, my life was severely limited.

An acquaintance declared he would pay for the babysitter if I would attend old time dances with him occasionally. Our friendship progressed. Many weeks later on my birthday, my escort presented me with a hearing device. WOW! What excitement for me to hear.

The world became brighter as my enthusiasm in being able to participate in activities nurtured talents heretofore hidden. My life opened up, personally, socially, musically, and financially. And certainly romantically for now I could *hear* his "sweet nothings."

Several months later our unusual square-dance wedding legally sealed our romance and I heard each word of the lovely ceremony and all the congratulations and conversations. This thoughtful, enlightened man brought love and security to me and mine for many years. Thank you for allowing me to share my romantic experience. ♡

See how just a little thing—a little risk—can change a life? It's amazing what a difference each one of us can make. All we have to do is forget about such things as obstacles and plunge onward to a lifetime of love. This, above all, is the lesson we can learn from Otha and Carolyn Lewis in their love story labeled:

A 30-YEAR HONEYMOON
by Mrs. Carolyn Lewis

My husband Otha B. Lewis is the most romantic man in the world. We married when I was 15 and he was 18 in spite of dire warnings of failure from everyone. "He won't be able to find a job to provide for you," they said. (He had lost his left leg in a crash at age 15.) But Otha did get a job and still works for the same company today.

In the first five years of marriage, we had four children. It was a struggle, but we were happy. He would manage to take me out on a "date" once a week and occasionally bring me little gifts, even though money was always scarce in the early years.

He was always happy to watch the kids for me so I could go window shopping or something when I needed a little while away. He was an excellent father and still is. All our children grew up healthy and happy and we have seven wonderful grandchildren. Otha was always there for them, and to me it made him so much more romantic because he is a warm and loving man, not only to our children, but to the rest of my family.

This year, he had flowers sent to me every single week of the year. That was his 29th anniversary present to me. He calls from work every day just to say he loves me and is thinking of me. He tells me I'm beautiful even though I'm fat and over 40, and when he says it he looks at me with so much love in his eyes he makes me believe it. It's been a 30-year honeymoon because of this wonderful man. ♡

Otha and Carolyn obviously know no obstacles to happiness. They've lived a life of happiness for almost 30 years. And thanks to their positive attitude, everything has worked out great. You could say the same about our last barrier-busters. They triumphed, and laughed, when they found themselves:

TICKLED BY LOVE
by Mrs. Kaye G.

Is there anyone who is happy? I recently underwent major surgery and, needless to say, this was a very traumatic experience for me and my family. I entered the hospital three days prior to surgery and it was indeed a "low" time. My husband, however, was thinking of my feelings, even though his spirits were quite low.

The morning before surgery I awoke at 7:30 and went over to the window from which I had a beautiful view. I opened the drapes and was extremely tickled and surprised at what greeted me. My room was on the second floor and, as I looked out the window, a huge helium-filled balloon with a "smiling face" was smiling at me. All around the balloon was written "I love you" and "Get well." Everyone thought it was such a romantic act on my husband's part, especially since we've been married 23 years. Of course, he also brought me the traditional flowers and candy. I must add that everything turned out great! ♡

You now know the answer to making your love stronger, too. Forget the word "obstacle." Ignore the idea of "barriers." And for God's sake, use a little less common sense.

Like every great lover in this book, you have the answers to your problems right there within you. Let Otha Lewis's success story show you the way. Let Sally Clayton's zest for life give you the energy to pull through. These ordinary loving folks have succeeded against all odds. And what they want you to know is that you can too.

Lovers—There Is More to Sex Than Butter-Flavor Crisco

With all the talk about *improving* sex nowadays you'd think that everyone's lovelife had gone to the dogs. Well, passion and adventure fans, it hasn't. In fact, things are far from a Toto failure in the Land of Ahhhs.

How come? Or, better yet, why? Because Americans have learned that there's more to sex than Butter-Flavor Crisco. They've learned that the secret to good sex is good romance. And you're about to learn that there are thousands of lovers—nay Virginia, ten times ten thousand lovers—out there who are surprisingly good at "it."

That doesn't really surprise you, does it? After all, you are one of these great lovers, right? Darned right. And now that we agree, let me tell you why you are so passionate.

1) Contrary to *Cosmo,* the sexual revolution hasn't passed you by. You know that men can and should be sensitive *and* strong, and that women can and should be assertive *and* feminine.

2) You have *always* known that variety is the spice of life and that no effort should be spared to keep your relationship new and exciting.

3) You've already heard every sex therapist describe in generic detail the various permutations and propositions that explain the *How's* of making love.

There's no doubt about it. You know "how" to be a truly great lover. What you may be missing, strangely enough, is the "why." The "Why should I be a great lover when: a) Even a small cry of passion might wake up one of the kids? b) A dinner by candlelight only means the electric bill is overdue again? or c) I'm so tired, when I tried to seductively throw myself on the bed I missed?"

Why be a great lover? Because a great love makes *everything* seem better. Scientists have shown that for people in great love, small paychecks seem bigger, noisy children seem quieter, and great efforts seem easier.

It takes one small effort to make all of this happen. All you have to do is forget the real world. Instead, create your own world where your great love can passionately exist.

That's what the following Great American Lovers have done. They know that the right atmosphere, not the latest technique, is the *one and only* secret to sexual success. They've put their faith in romance, and that faith has been rewarded over and over again.

Of course, things don't always work out as planned. P. T. Thompson, for example, made every mistake in the book of love. But thanks to some planning and good luck, she sent her lovelife soaring in a hot-blooded story she called:

THE NIGHT MODESTY BLAZED
by P. T. Thompson

Actually, I don't suppose I was born shy. I think it was just an affliction I developed after being married for over 20 years and then suddenly finding myself single at age 39. It took almost two more years, full of constant encouragement from my daughter Chris and my friends, to finally make it out into the world of dating.

Then, in the fall of 1984, I met Dennis. It's funny, but when I look back in my journal to the entry I made after our first date, there was only one line written, "This man is really weird." Well, in a way I guess that sort of comes close to the truth because from what I've seen and been told, men like Dennis are few and far between nowadays.

I rapidly became spoiled to all the flowers and cards he gave me and to all the meals he prepared for me just because he enjoyed doing it. But, after dating for almost three months, I had yet to make a meal for him. So I decided after the holidays, I was going to make it up to him for all the wonderful things he had been doing for me all these months.

I carefully planned a simple but elegant seafood dinner with a scallop casserole, small tossed salad, chilled white wine, candles, linen napkins and my body—dressed in nothing but a black lace teddy and a small red apron. Oh, and of course I shouldn't forget the sexy, black three-inch high heels and about six yards of leg.

I worked like a little beaver all day Saturday, cooking and cleaning and trying to get everything prepared ahead of time so that while he waited for his dinner, all I had to do was bend seductively over the oven a few times while the casserole was cooking. I was so nervous at the thought of trying to cook and be sexy at the same time that twice that day I burned the scallops and had to throw out the whole mess, run to the store, buy more scallops and start all over from scratch.

Finally, the time for my romantic little dinner for two was at hand. Ah, the atmosphere was perfect and the smells coming from the kitchen were heaven scent. Now all I needed was my Lochinvar—my knight in shining armor. Nervously, I paced the floor watching the clock, waiting for the doorbell to ring.

At last—the doorbell. I quickly checked the mirror one last time (wetting my lips just the way Marilyn Monroe used to do in all her movies). Slowly, I opened the door, striking the most seductive pose I could muster up and, to my eternal surprise and embarrassment, heard—

"Oh, hi Mom. Just thought I'd bring back the vacuum cleaner I borrowed last wee—Holy cow

Mother! Where's your clothes? Oh gee. I'm so sorry. Ha, ha. Oh Mother. Ha, ha, ha, ha. Gosh. Ha, ha. I forgot. Ha, ha. Dennis was coming for dinner. I really am sorry. Ha, ha!"

Standing directly behind my now hysterical daughter was, of course, Dennis who had arrived just in time to see my flaming face and utter panic at trying to cover myself up in front of my daughter. While I stood there, silently praying for the world to come to an end, Dennis quietly stepped inside smiling at me and said nothing.

Meanwhile, my daughter Chris quickly put the vacuum cleaner away and after greeting Dennis turned to leave. On her way to the door, she stopped, walked over to me with a huge grin, hugged me tight and whispered in my ear, "By the way Mom, you look terrific!" With that, the door closed behind her and she was gone.

I turned and looked at Dennis, who still hadn't said a word to me. My face, which had changed from deep scarlet to dusty rose, flushed again as he walked up, put his arms around me and said,

"Hi beautiful, what's cookin'? Whatever it is, it can't be any better than what I'm holding in my arms right now." ♡

Ah yes, the joys of being a mom. (By the way, how many of you out there are named "Mom"? Doesn't it get confusing?) Sometimes it's so joy-filled it makes you want to turn in your National Stretch Mark membership card. That is, until your offspring do something so wonderful and so helpful that you just want to buy them a case of Twinkies. Such was the case when—in search of tips on how to be a great lover—I asked a group of fourth graders to give me their secrets to the first and most important step in Crisco-free lovemaking, *The Kiss*. They called their handy, and unedited, hints:

STEP ONE—PUCKER UP REAL GOOD
by Miss Margolis's Fourth-Grade Class

Jason: "1) Get close up. 2) Make sure the other person doesn't have a toilet plunger in his/her hand. 3) Pucker up. 4) Take caution. 5) KISS. 6) Don't get stuck. 7) Pull apart."

Kristina: "This is how they kiss on soap operas: First they get close, then they open their mouths and put their lips together, and make nasty noises. This is how my Mom and Dad kiss: First my Dad comes home from work. My Mom comes up to him and says 'I missed you, Honey' and then puckers up her lips and kisses my Dad. It does *not* sound nasty."

Adam: "Step 1) Pucker up real good. Step 2) Touch lips. Step 3) Pull apart lips. Step 4) Make smacking noise. Hugging and kissing is a sign of pure LOVE. Caution—Remove lips at same time or someone will kiss air."

Andrea: "First you open your arms wide in slow motion. Then you get close to one another. After that you fling your arms around the person. Then you pucker up your lips. Then you put both of your lips together. For how to combine kissing and hugging, first you take your girlfriend/wife to a drive-in movie. Then you wrap your arms around her. Then you take your mouth and put your lips together."

Jule: "Instructions for Grownup Kissing. 1) Close your eyes. 2) Tilt your head. 3) Girls put your arms around his neck. 4) Boys put your arms around her waist. 5) Pucker up and . . . 6) ZOWIE!"

Amy: "How you hug is you get face to face with who you are hugging and you smack your head on their shoulder. Then you put your arms around them and they put their arms around your neck. How you kiss is you put your mouth to their mouth. Then make a fish mouth."

David: "1) Close your eyes. 2) Put your arms around each other. 3) Get closer. 4) Put your lips together. NOW YOU KNOW."

Patrick: "Step 1. Go up to somebody when they least expect it. 2. Lock your arms around their waist. 3. Turn the person around. 4. Squeeze them."

Felicia: "Get sick then you don't have to kiss that person." ♡

Let's see, so far you've learned how to embarrass yourself by showing up nearly naked at the front door, and you've also discovered, and not a moment too soon, that you should check your partner for a plunger before puckering. Well, it looks like we're really making progress. And speaking of progress, if we're going to make you an even greater lover in this chapter, we'd better get in gear. We'd better jump-start the Mr. Romance instructional series known as . . .

How To Make Love Like a Buick

First Gear—Getting Things Rolling

The strangest things can get lovers' libidos leaping. A sniff of passionate perfume. A touch of sensuous silk. A taste of tuna salad sandwich. Give 'em that little kick to get things started and then get ready for flaming passion (or at least be prepared to hose 'em down).

So, what exactly do you rub together to create the immortal romance flambé? In first gear they suggest nibbling on:

A Little Fried Chickadee
by Wesley of Mesa, Arizona

My wife is the true romantic. She surprises me by calling and leaving cute little messages with my secretary or, better yet, she calls at quitting time with some good ideas. The best one is at the end of the day when I answer the phone and the sexy "Mae West" at the other end of the line says, "Hey, big man, my husband isn't home. Why don't you drop by and see me?" Then she proceeds to give me our address. Someday I will get a speeding ticket as I hurry home. ♡

Yes reader, think of Wesley the next time you see someone with a grin the size of W. C. Fields go zipping by. And—in case you glimpse a tractor breaking the land romance record—you'll know it's time to be on the lookout for:

4-SIDNEY-0, THE MAD CB'ER OF SIDNEY, OHIO
by (who else?) "4-Sidney-0"

In our games at noon—occasionally, but always when I know her chores are the heaviest—I set up the following for my wife and lover (same person). I have a secret picnic prepared with wine, cheese and a loaf of bread, and then ask my wife, via a CB radio on my tractor, to meet me in OUR haystack at noon. Needless to say, romance is queen—and king—for a wonderful love break. And a lot of the early afternoon is spent blissfully picking bits of hay off each other's person and forgetting the mundane before the kids get home. ♡

A loaf of bread, a jug of wine . . . and zow! Kind of

gives a whole new meaning to the phrase "a roll in the hay," don't you think?

And while Sidney and his wife choose straws for romance, Mrs. Arlene Angelo heads straight for the bottle, the perfume bottle that is. Her brief story of sweet-smelling success is called:

A FEW DROPS OF LOVE

I drop several drops of perfume on the pillows and sheets before we retire. My husband is 81 and I am 71, but we do maintain sexual relations—almost weekly. We thank the good Lord for our health and enjoyment. ♡

And in response to Arlene, a fun-loving woman named Ruth wrote:

A FEW DROPS OF LUNCH

After reading your column about the 71-year-old lady who sprinkled drops of perfume on the pillow at night to create an aura for romance, we regretted that we are *both* allergic to perfume. But because my husband loves the smell of chocolate, I chose a dark-colored pillow-case, rubbed a small amount of baking chocolate inside the case and guess what?

No, you're wrong. We laughed so hard we were too exhausted for romance. We giggled for hours. And we are not youngsters, either. ♡

Quit giggling and shift your gears. It's time for:

SECOND GEAR—PICKING UP SPEED

If you're looking to go even faster than high-speed baking chocolate, then it's time to be exotic, erotic and tricky. It's time to *plan* for a little sensual spontaneity and romance-inspiring atmosphere, as in this letter entitled:

SURPRISE, SURPRISE, SURPRISE
by Roger Fulton

My very romantic wife recently pulled a trick on me (romantic, of course) that I have to share with you. After spending six months overseas away from my family, I recently returned home and received a very un-expected surprise. About the third or fourth night back, she sent me off on a grocery store errand. This was somewhat unusual and on the way back home, I wondered if she might be cooking up some surprise. Did she ever.

On the front door was a sign directing me to come in and go over to the stereo. By the stereo was a sign telling me to be seated, make myself comfortable, and hit PLAY on the tape deck. I wasn't sure what was coming up, but I could hardly wait to find out. As soon as the music began, my wife slinked out through the kitchen door into the living room. She was wearing an incredibly exotic and enticing belly-dancing costume that about popped my eyes right out of my head. I usually don't appreciate being fooled, but this kind of fooling I'll take any day. ♡

And speaking of fooling, how about:

A MAIDENFORM FOOL FOR LOVE
by Anne Monateri

Our romantic story starts at a dinner party during a past Christmas season. Everyone was asked to tell their romantic fantasy. When it came to my turn, I said I would like to pick up my husband after work in a white fur coat and limo (a la the Maidenform ad.)

Guess what? For my birthday my husband Vince surprised me with a knee-length white fur coat. Now it was my turn to surprise him. It took a lot of planning but I was able to pull it off. The limo pulled up outside Vince's office and I walked in with a red rose, a bottle of champagne and a hotel room key. And we left.

I'm still grinning as I write this and it's been over a year since we had our weekend. It was one of the greatest adventures of our lives. ♡

OK, OK, so not everyone can afford a white fur coat, a limo and a year-long grin. How about buying a scanty piece of feminine material that wraps gently around your femur? How about:

DON'T MIND IF THIGH DO
by Shirley Cohen

To keep the spark alive in our marriage, once a year I surprise my husband by wearing a garter as I did on our wedding night. I never wear it on the same occasion, so he never knows when he'll get one. He now has 12, for we celebrated our 13th anniversary in February. ♡

See now, wasn't that simple? Clothes—or the lack thereof—can really help your lovelife pick up speed. In fact, amorous apparel can even rocket your romance back to the future as in this letter quaintly called:

GIVING IT THE OLD VICTORIAN VA-VA-VA-VOOM
by Robert Munson

In a recent column you asked readers to write and tell you of their ideas of a wild and crazy romantic time. I doubt our idea would be considered wild, but many undoubtedly consider it crazy.

My wife is a dedicated career woman in a high-pressure administrative position, while I fight the bureaucratic hassles of public service on a daily basis. Our lives are hectic in the extreme, so for romance we drop out of the 20th Century completely.

For romance we become totally Victorian in terms of clothing, actions, mannerisms, and whenever possible, setting. My wife Carol Anne exchanges her business suits for the frills, lace and hoops of the 1860's. I go from uniform and badge to cutaway or frock coat.

Of an evening we will go to a period restaurant in which decor and service are strictly 19th Century, for an intimate dinner, followed by waltzing at home. For weekends, we visit a period-style hotel or bed-and-breakfast, again to allow our setting and behavior follow the gentle, relaxed and refined manners of the Victorians.

In keeping with the period, we often leave our hostelry after breakfast for a long stroll in the woods (or in earlier days when we lived near the sea, along the beach) and then a picnic. Flirting under the moonlight again is a sweet, gentle passion.

Oftentimes our relations are no more intimate than lacing up her corset; dressing and undressing with Victorian discretion can be more inflammatory than blatant exposure. The Victorians were well aware of the value of imagination in sex appeal. Undressing a Victorian lady's many layers of clothing can draw out anticipation to an exquisite degree, like a child opening a multiple nested egg at Christmas. ♡

Ho, ho, ho.

THIRD GEAR—ZOOMING ALONG

So, how do you like your Buick so far? It may not be the latest model, but just wait until you see how it handles the curves in:

A Red Ribbon Winner
by "Young at Heart" from Green Valley, Arizona

We're still romantic after 50 years! My husband and I went on a Caribbean cruise this spring to celebrate our 50th anniversary. Imagine my concern when I realized I had left his gift at home. When we docked at an island, I bought some pretty red satin ribbon.

The night of our anniversary, I draped the red ribbon around just me and tied a gorgeous big bow in front. I walked into the bedroom and said, "Ta-da, here's your gift honey! I didn't forget." He was speechless. It must have rekindled that old spark, as his eyes lit up just like on our honeymoon. P.S. You don't print names, do you? If you do, burn this up. I'd die of mortification. ♡

Also not willing to die of mortification is the semi-anonymous J. K. from Hillsboro, Missouri, who countered with:

How to Put a Ribbon on It

My wife and I heard this joke: "First lady: What did your husband give you for your anniversary? Second lady: The same old thing, but with a ribbon on it." So, on our anniversary, when my wife came to bed she found I had put a ribbon around myself. We've had a lot of laughs about that. Seriously, though: We consider ourselves to be gifts to each other, so why not gift-wrap yourself for your spouse? You may have to use a little imagination to figure out how to attach the ribbon, but it's worth it. ♡

Also worth "it" is the prospect of being caught with your romance down. But beware: This sort of third-gear surprise is for experts only, like the following woman who wrote:

THE SURPRISE OF HIS WIFE
by Robin Blakely

Several years ago, and shortly after the birth of our second child, our marriage was very ordinary and even teetering on boredom. I knew something had to be done. So with a little help from my parents, I set a secret plan into action: to have a surprise meeting at one of our local hotels.

This took considerable planning and scheming to pull off. First, I had to make sure that I had a sitter for the kids. Next I set my plan in motion and contacted the hotel of my choice and explained my scheme to a very understanding clerk.

My plan was to get my husband to the hotel under false pretenses. His being in the flower business made this task a little easier. I rented a room under a false name and then made arrangements for my husband to make an "emergency" delivery to the name I had registered under.

When my husband arrived, he was not in a very good

mood because he is not fond of making deliveries. To make matters worse, when he got to the hotel desk he was told he would have to deliver the package to the room himself.

Meanwhile, I was in the room waiting with a bottle of champagne and a cheese tray. When he showed up at our room and I opened the door in a very sexy nightie, his mouth hit the floor. At first he thought he had "caught" me, but when he realized it was an evening for just the two of us, he loved it. It truly was an evening of romance. ♡

And if you think that sensual surprise took passionate planning, then you'll marvel at the magnificent:

WHO'S THAT ON MY PILLOW?
WHY, IT'S THE TOOTH FAIRY
by Andrew Kassman

This letter is dedicated to my wife, Terry, the only woman who could have changed my life so much in such a short time. I don't know where to begin. I'm about to leave on a trip and whenever I go away alone I get flowers in my room (to keep me thinking of her, as if I could forget). I also always get love notes in my socks—they would easily make the best seller list in some juicy, sexy novel—she's probably doing that right now. (That's why she insists on packing my underwear.)

But I'll tell you, birthdays are her specialty. On one of my birthdays, Terry hired an entire 75-piece high-school marching band to play all my favorite tunes at my office. On my next birthday, I was followed all day by the Tooth Fairy (I'm an orthodontist). My wife hired an actress to come to my office for lunch and take me to a fancy restaurant where she met us with two little twin blonde fairies. Then, the head fairy returned in the afternoon to give me 20 pounds of chocolate.

The next birthday, as I walked into my office, I was greeted by my two employees dressed in Maid Marian princess outfits. They were waiting to put on my robe and crown. I was made King for a Day. I was never so admired and felt so high and mighty—it was how Terry always felt about me. In the afternoon I had a three-piece ensemble of trumpets playing for me while a woman read from a scroll granting me my new kingdom. That evening we went out and Terry hired a magician to do tricks at our table. I was still dressed up. And later, we had an even more wonderful time. ♡

I mean really, can you imagine a group of 75 champagne music-makers oompah-ing in your office parking lot? Why that's—dare I say it—wunnerful, wunnerful, wunnerful.

AND NOW, FOURTH GEAR: OVERDRIVE

By now you've discovered the method to this chapter's madness. Instead of telling you what I think is the "perfect" way to promote passion, I've let you read what the real experts have to say. And while you may think that some of their stories are as erotic as an iced waterbed, you can't fault them for trying.

The message here is simple: All you have to do is try. If you want a lot of great sex, you have to give it some good effort. You have to make sure that your romance is:

ALL LUBED UP & READY TO GO

As a baby-boomer, I grew up during the era captured in our now oldies but goodies—"Why Do I Fall in Love," "Papa's Got a Brand New Baby," and "Baby Love." Unfortunately, I couldn't truly experience that rich musical and vibrant period due to a very strict and protected upbringing coupled with my father's constant reassignment from one small, out-of-the-way air base to another.

I often fantasized about how things would have felt romantically—going steady, that first real kiss, and "parking" after a dance. I met Vincent last summer. He, too, is a baby-boomer. Some of his funniest escapades are naturally from his teenage years. I would intentionally jog a story out of ol' Vince about one of his teenage loves to try to vicariously relive his date's feelings and thoughts at the moment he tried to first kiss her or even "cop a feel."

After we dated for a while, he rang me at work and

made a special date. Vince asked me to wear my long jean skirt and loafers. That evening, to my surprise, he showed up in his brother's '64 Corvette wearing jeans, his old Alpha Phi Alpha fraternity sweater, and playing taped music of Wolfman Jack's oldies show. Of course, we did a nostalgic trip that evening by eating at McDonald's, snacking at Dairy Queen, and then going for a drive with the top down to a secluded overlook where we parked.

I could end this letter by saying that we "made out," but that wouldn't do Vince justice. He went one step further than just recreating a missing part of my younger years. He sincerely reproduced his manners, actions and fears that he had known at "those moments." The uncertainty of putting his arm around me, the nervous chatter while testing for the right moment to kiss, the trembling hand on the knee, and, most of all, that quiet moment of solace and guilt shared and felt by both after they had "gone all the way"—or mighty close to it— back in those days. ♡

Yes, the good old days of sex. A time when the words "romantic interlude" meant more than a station break during *The Tonight Show*. A time when there was more to making love than perspiration.

You can bring those days back—like all of our great American lovers have—by not worrying about having "good sex." Spend your time, instead, planning "good romance." Here's your passion checklist:

☐ Item #1: Have I included an element of surprise? (Mysterious phone calls, out-of-the-ordinary gifts, surprisingly little clothing.)

☐ Item #2: Have I added a breath of fresh romantic atmosphere? (Fragrant flowers, flickering candles, mighty Mr. Bubble.)

☐ Item #3: Have I made it easy to have fun? (Private location, relaxed itinerary, a bottle of champagne.)

☐ Item #4: Have I forgotten the real world? (No mention of mortgages, no talk of children, no giggling as my partner undresses.)

☐ Item #5: Have I brought along my trusty sense of humor? (A smile is my umbrella, a grin is my overcoat, a laugh is my lingerie.)

Yes, passionate reader, your great lovelife is waiting. You already know "how." You now know "why." And, after you spend a little time planning, you'll certainly know "when." So where do you begin? Well, our great lovers say that there is no place like home to kick up your heels and create your very own Land of Ahhhs.

Parents—
Toys and Tricycles
Are
Terrific Titillators

Only parents know the true impact of *romancus interruptus,* that much-feared moment when—in the midst of parental cuddling—a tiny voice says, "Mommy, Daddy, don't get up. Just tell me how to get blood stains out of the living room carpet."

Ah, children. Ah, families. Ah, shucks. It's no wonder that 98.6 percent of hot-blooded American parents believe that "real" romance is destined to end when the family begins.

Well, passion and pablum fans, can you guess what America's Greatest Lovers have to say to that? If you picked "Bushwah!" you're right on the mark. These romantics fervently believe that love is an even better bargain when it comes at group rates.

You're not convinced? I'm not surprised. The third most frequent question sent to me through my newspaper column is "How can a couple be romantic when they have little money and loads of kids?" (What are questions 1 and 2 you ask? "Where and how can a single woman find a man?" and "How can I jump-start my husband?") Obviously, the secrets to passionate parenthood are still a mystery to most of us. Let it be so no longer:

THREE SECRETS TO BEING
A ROMANTIC MOMMY OR DADDY
(AS REVEALED BY AMERICA'S GREATEST LOVERS)

1) Absolutely ignore your children.

Kids love to watch their folks be romantic. And why not? Whenever a mommy kisses a daddy it tells a child that "everything is OK." They love to know that. You love to do it, so go ahead. Get romantic (within reason) in front of your children. In fact, ignore them. Forget that they are there. Your romance and family will thank you.

2) Coerce your children into being romantic too.

Kids, especially young ones, like to be helpful. They throw you a blowdryer when you are in the tub. They clean your car's upholstery with their own tube of toothpaste. And they cheerfully pull out all of those "funny-looking weeds" from your herb garden. The darlings.

You can channel all of this helpful energy into helpful romance by making your offspring part of your passion. For example, one extraordinarily creative woman dressed her children as waiters and had them serve a mess-free candlelit dinner. And as you're about to read, many other couples found romance when they included their children in a portion of their amorous activities.

3) Dads make or break passionate parenting.

Let me be blunt: If your romance flew out the window when the stork came by, chances are that Dad is the only one who can reclaim it. It's a fact that 99% of American mothers are ready, willing and able to be romantic, provided they have a little help from their mates. And, as you're about to read, it doesn't take much. All a guy has to do is help with the housework, bring home a flower, or even cook up:

A BOWL OF TEARWATER CHILI
by Karen Pence

Recently my husband Vic had to be out of town for a few weeks, only coming home on every other weekend. Not only did he call home every night, he wrote letters, cards and even brought me home a teddy bear.

While he was home one weekend, our three youngest daughters and I had to leave for a few hours. When we returned he had set the table very romantically, even using candles. He had made his "famous" chili. When we sat down, he asked to say something to us before we ate. He told us that all the time he had been preparing the meal tears kept coming to his eyes when he thought of how much he had and how lucky he was to have me and four beautiful daughters, and how being gone had brought him a new appreciation of us.

Telling this, he began to let tears stream down his face. Seeing this, the rest of us began to cry so we all sat there holding hands and salting our chili. We named it "tearwater chili."

That is not an isolated incident. He brings home flowers, perfume, cards and gifts—just because. He never fails to make me feel like I'm "First Lady" and he also treats his daughters to individual special dinners, brings them home carnations, treats, and loves to take us all out to nice restaurants. He's not only a great husband, lover, father and best friend, he's also our knight in shining armor. There need to be more REAL men like him in this world and I think he's number one and richly deserves to be recognized. ♡

A *real* real man. Not just the guy who pumps aluminum at the Arnold Schwarzenegger Memorial Bar and Grill, but the kind of man who isn't afraid to openly care for his family—a man like John Ball. His daughters described him this way:

NO COMPLAINTS ABOUT OUR FAB DAD
by Rebecca, Jennifer and Christie Ball

We think our dad is the world's greatest lover because

he is loving, kind, sincere, cheerful, helpful, and always there when we need him.

For example, when he's worked all day, he comes home and my mom runs him across town to visit friends and he *never* complains. We will come home and he fixes dinner and never complains. Then at least one of us will have him help us with homework, which takes about two hours and still he never complains. He has always been there for us since we can always remember.

When we told him we had to have new dresses for the dance he never complained about where the money would come from, he just asked when we had to have them. He *always* has time to listen to our problems or just listen to our silly jokes. (He always laughs and sometimes they aren't that funny.) If we are sick, he's the first one to make sure we are covered up.

He has this beeper and no matter when we beep him he doesn't ever get mad, even if it's just to bring our curling iron because we forgot it and are spending the night at a friend's house. There are a thousand stories we could tell, but the important one is that we love and appreciate our dad. ♡

OK men, confess. How many of you—without complaint—would willingly be beeped for a curling iron? I think I can safely say that Mr. Ball should be uniquely commended for a job above and beyond the call of beauty.

And he's not alone. Fully aware of secret 3 to fabulous family romance (and secrets 1 and 2) is the entire Wingle clan. Their soaring story is called:

ON THE WINGLES OF ROMANCE
by Carla Wingle

I am sending in my ballot for the romantic of the year award. I think it should go to Leonard and Carla Wingle and their children as the nation's "Most Romantic Family." Leonard and Carla have three very romantic children, Angela, 8, Kenneth, 6, and Pamela, 4. On New Year's Eve, Leonard and Carla wanted to go out, but not without their children. So they found a roller rink that was having a New Year's party and took the whole family. At midnight, Leonard skated with Angela and she said, "When I go to school I'm telling everyone I skated with my daddy at midnight." Isn't that romantic?

One day the parents took Pamela grocery shopping, and while walking down the aisle she just stopped and exclaimed, "I love you, Mom!" Now, isn't that romantic?

On Carla's birthday the little ones wanted to give her breakfast in bed, so she got up and helped them make it—and then she went back to bed and pretended to be sleeping. The children were so excited that they could give their mom breakfast in bed. Now, isn't that romantic? ♡

Yes, darn it, that's romantic—for mom, for dad and

for the kids. It's also important. It's important for us to realize that *everyone* benefits from each show of love. This is also the moving message of Robin Everett in her story dubbed:

ROCKING CHAIR LOVE
by Robin Everett

Love and romance is expressed in so many ways in this family. My husband and I have been married almost four years and we have two sons ages 3 years and 18 months. I'll be sitting there watching Sesame Street with our three-year-old and he will look up at me and say "I love you, Mommy."

When my husband comes in from work, our 18-month-old will point to the rocking chair for him to sit down. Then my husband puts some soft music on the radio, holds them both in his arms and talks to them about their day. After dinner we give them a bath and put them to bed, then read them a bedtime story or just make one up. This is followed by lots of hugs and kisses. My husband's and my time alone is spent cuddling and talking. We love each other very much and it shows in our children. ♡

Showing your affection. That's the key to a happy family and a revved-up romance. The trick is in knowing when, where and—especially—how much to show. For the answer, check out this story called:

A REVEALING RECIPE FOR YOUR RELATIONSHIP
by Mindy T. from Wichita, Kansas

I've always felt that if romance is a top priority (as it should be), you will make the time. Our two children know that when the door's closed, it's Mommy and Daddy's close time. They respect this and we never have any hassles. Some evenings I will even ask a friend to keep our kids. Believe me, when my husband walks in to a wife cooking in only an apron, it is definitely worth the effort. (Mr. Romance Note: Just stay away from frying greasy foods.)

We also make a point of going to a motel every month or so. Our favorite summer motel is our tent. Between wine, cheese, moonlight and the lake, WOW. I dare anybody out there to tell me romance isn't worth a little extra effort. ♡

So, what does a little extra romantic effort sometimes get you? "Pregnant," you reply expectantly. Yes indeed. Making romance can lead to making babies, which leads to making love.

If you'll allow me to jump back in time a bit—to the months *before* the birth of the baby—I'd like to show how some creative couples have kept romance alive in their relationships when they found pregnancy in their family way. We begin with a hefty heart-warmer called:

30 POUNDS OF GLOW
by "Super Dad's Wife in Ohio"

During my pregnancy I remember those "glorious" days when I simply thought the mirror was my worst enemy. Yet all through those times my husband was my life-support system by being my best friend, and telling me how great I looked and how much I turned him on with that "pregnant glow." (Believe me, I had more than a glow. About 30 pounds more.)

I was worried that my big basketball exterior would totally exclude me from feeling romantic. I was terribly worried we would grow farther apart as I grew bigger around. But even those days and nights when I did feel less romantic and beautiful my wonderful husband and I found many ways to deal with my "curvatures," or should I say, my *new* curvatures.

I learned that mothers-to-be should praise their husbands because they can prove to be the best thing or person to help you get through your special time together. A simple hug at an unexpected moment, a call at work just to say, "Hi, I love you," seem to mean a hundred times more than usual when you're both kind of on edge anticipating the special delivery.

Pregnancy is also a great time to discover some of the other sides of your romantic relationship. Making an elegant candlelight dinner, then dancing close to each other is great (the closer the better, if possible).

But sometimes, yes, during pregnancy, you have a *giant* craving for a more passionate evening. Never give up. Look around. Believe me, there *are* sexy nighties you can fit into. And even if you don't feel like Miss Universe, your husband will be "aroused" by your courage to put it on. ♡

Courage. To fight for your place as King (or Queen) of the forest. Courage. To fight for romance when your skin is the sorest. Ahem. As in this story called:

WHAT'S SHAMU WITH YOU?
by "Soft as a Baby's Behind" from Wickliffe, Ohio

Here are a few things my husband did to keep us both happy during my pregnancy. First of all, from the day I found out I was pregnant, my sweet man would rub baby oil on my stomach and back. This may not sound like much, but toward the end of my pregnancy I was very uncomfortable. You see, I was carrying *twins* and my skin had to stretch quickly so the oil made me feel much better.

Along with the oil, I'll always remember a day around my sixth month. I was feeling especially down (you know, like someone had just mistaken me for Shamu the Killer Whale) and my dear sweet husband tied a ten pound bag of potatoes around his neck, put on a big shirt, and had me sit down at the table while he struggled and bounced around the kitchen to make our lunch. If that wasn't enough to make me laugh, he dropped something and squatted down to pick it up. I laughed so hard I thought my water would break!

Needless to say, we had a very nice lunch. And, thanks to my husband, I don't have "twin skin," but we do have two beautiful healthy boys. ♡

I may be wrong, but I think there's another message for us here. And no, it's not that oil can grease up your romance. This time the message reads: The strongest love—and the strongest passion—is found in the strongest families.

Instead of just looking *outside* the family for romance ("Gosh we could start having fun if only we got away for a week"), it's time we started looking *inside* our families for love. Sure, it's great to get away and just be a wild and crazy couple again. And I recommend you do that as often as possible. But the passionate truth is that those chances are few and far between.

Much more common are those little moments that show you love *and* are willing to pamper your partner, even with Pampers-wearing pipsqueaks around. Just ask Gloria Villegas. She wrote:

MY, HOW TIME FLU
by Gloria Villegas

My husband Danny has shown me in countless ways how much he loves me. Shortly after our marriage I became pregnant, but it resulted in a miscarriage. Danny held my hand throughout the ordeal—the hemorrhaging, the pain and finally the D and C.

Two months later I became pregnant again and he went to *every* visit to the doctor with me—often he was the only male in a waiting room full of women. And yes, we went through childbirth-training classes together and the birth of our baby, cesarean section. I'll never forget the look on this man's face when the doctor handed him his nine-pound, seven-ounce son; Danny beamed.

I realize that in this day and age this is not uncommon, but I know of few men who would give up two weeks' vacation—two years going—in order to help change the babies' diapers, feed, clothe and bathe them, do housework and cook meals. (We had another son 16 months later.)

Now we have been married six years and Danny is *still* mopping floors, cleaning bathrooms, going grocery shopping, doing laundry, folding it, putting it away in drawers, tucking the kids into bed, preparing lunches, getting up in the middle of the night whenever one of the kids wants a glass of water, and making sure the kids' blankets are covering them instead of in a bundle at the foot of the bed. Several months ago we *all* caught the flu and felt equally miserable, but there were still meals to cook, laundry to wash, groceries to be bought—and who do you suppose mustered up enough strength to get it all done? Danny. He's the best and I'm so blessed. Just thought you might like to know. ♡

60

You might also like to know about the strong family love shared by the Robert Stevens family. Mrs. Stevens wrote:

LOVE FROM THE TIPS OF OUR TOES
by Susan Stevens

I could tell you about all the wild sexual fantasies that my husband Robert has sweetly, lovingly and considerately fulfilled over the years. I could tell you about how tender and thoughtful he is or how he lights up my heart just by walking into the room. But these things are such a very small part of what the man I call my husband is all about.

Robert is a man who takes pleasure in scrubbing the baby's knees and feet in the bathtub after the baby has had a hard day racing Mom to whatever he *isn't* supposed to have. Robert is a man who makes a delightful game for the baby out of the grueling task of physical therapy. This is also a man who smilingly lifts his three-year-old daughter on his shoulders at the airport so she can be the first to see Grandma when she comes to visit and makes an adventure for this three-year-old out of the Sunday morning funnies as they bounce together on our waterbed. And here is also a man who has done his best to be a friend as well as a guide to his two step-children, ages 12 and 14.

In addition to all this, Robert has never complained about the *four* hours driving time to his job. Instead, he tells me how he never tires of the scenery, of watching the wildlife change and grow. He always somehow manages to make the best out of a bad situation and it shows in his family life as well as his job.

Is he perfect? Not completely, but I'll save that side for when you ask for the "World's Biggest Jerk" stories. Is he the greatest? Well, I not only love Robert, I'm still "in love" with him—and I don't know of too many things greater than that. ♡

So, how do you build such a great family love? You work at it—along with generous time off for hanky panky. This has been the secret of success for none other than the original:

MR. & MRS. HANKY PANKY
by Jeanne Miller

My mother, Mrs. Bob (Ree) Miller, is the happiest and most romantic woman in the world. I asked my mother once if it was sad driving from Ohio directly after their wedding all the way to California where she knew no one and where she would be 3,000 miles away from her family. Without hesitation she replied: "No. You see, I would have followed your Dad anywhere. I didn't care where his job took him. I just wanted to be with him."

Twenty-eight years of marriage have not dimmed their love.

During my home visits from college I would still accidentally stumble upon Mom and Dad kissing by the stairs. They still go out on dates, and we five kids, now grown, echo what they used to tell us; "Goodbye and have fun, but be back by 10:00 PM and no hanky-panky!" Mom puts on a crestfallen face and sighs sadly, "No hanky-panky? Ah, that's no fun."

They still call each other by affectionate nicknames, "Ange," short for Angel, meaning my mother, and "Nobber," of unknown origins, meaning my father. Once, in a pizza parlor, Mom triumphantly produced a bottle of champagne she had hidden in her purse, and she and Dad dined elegantly on pizza and champagne. To celebrate their 25th anniversary, Dad took the family to a music hall and gave Mom a 50-foot banner that announced in foot-high letters and became the hit of the theater, "THANKS, ANGE, FOR TWENTY-FIVE YEARS OF HAPPINESS. CAN I HAVE TWENTY-FIVE MORE?" Mom, with tears in her eyes, promised him fifty. ♡

A promise of love. A promise of passion. Can they be fulfilled when you live with ever-present pee wees? Sure they can. But it may take a change of perspective like the one detailed in this chapter's final letter:

WHEN YOU WISH UPON A BUG
by Lori Bower

So, you're looking for a great romance story? I have a story for you. Probably not your torrid, endless-nights-of-passion type, but a romance nonetheless.

We are romantic and loving and have children. Yes, children. You romantic? Your husband romantic? With children? You bet. We are as romantic as we can be with three children, a dog and a house full of bustling friends and neighbors.

Some people would say the party's over after you have kids, but we just say it's easier to have a party with five people. Don't get me wrong. I love parties of two also. But these are usually unplanned and unexpected. The flowers are few and far between, but the chocolate (which he knows I love) is plentiful. The fun really begins, though, after the kids are down for the night. It's midnight kitchen raids and talking till three. Sometimes other fun things, too.

With a good guy for a husband, you can be romantically in love after children. Things of course have changed some. When we were dating it was midnight strolls, looking at the stars and sharing our dreams. Now, we take daytime strolls, look at the bugs and share our new dreams with three old dreams come to pass.

I love the relationship my husband and I share. It's the man who can be a lover, father, and friend and yet still be himself that allows me to be myself. And it's by being ourselves and sharing all we have that allows us to be Great American Romantics. ♡

Again, these are the secrets:
1) Show love in front of your children.

2) Let your strong family build strong passion.
3) And help Dad be the good guy he really can be.

'Nuff said.

Kids Say the Most Romantic Things

I always liked the Art Linkletter show. Sitting in front of the tube, wearing my PF Flyers, I always wished Art would ask me to say the darndest things. Nobody ever did. But the thought of how much a ten-year-old mind really knows stuck with me. And, later, when I needed someone to tell me the innermost secrets to the romantic universe, I remembered Art.

So, after lacing up my Nikes (some things do change), I visited classroom after classroom full of fourth-graders. I asked them questions and they gave me more—and better—answers than I thought possible. It was the darndest thing.

I started with the simple, "How do you know your parents love each other?" and ended with the question that has perplexed seers, sages and slimeballs throughout the ages: "What is love?" Here—in lightly edited form with original errors and misspellings left intact for full romantic effect—is what these American fourth-graders had to say.

I KNOW MY PARENTS LOVE EACH OTHER WHEN . . .

Frankly, most adults have a hard time showing their love. And these same folks have a *really* hard time understanding when love is being shown to them. Not kids, though. They know just when their parents truly love each other:

Patrick: "Well every time my Dad comes home he always gets my Mom from behind, puts his hands around her waist, picks her up, takes her back into the bedroom. Next thing I know the shower's running." (I asked Patrick if he was serious and he said, "I'm serious as a heart attack.")

David: "When I go into their room to use our computer, they send me out, close the door and then I hear 'M-M-M-Smooch.' But I don't mind that because it tells me that they like each other a lot and I'm happy to hear that because that's friends."

James: "A lot of times on the weekends they go to bed before me and my brother do."

Jorge: "They go out a lot and I don't really mind it because I just sit down and watch TV. And then they come back happy."

I KNOW MY PARENTS LOVE ME BECAUSE . . .

If you think that a once-a-year Cub Scout outing or

the latest and greatest Christmas gift is enough to show children your love, you're wrong. They know that the real meaning of love is in the little things you do for them. They know that the real meaning of love is shown by your commitment to them over time. They know their parents love them because:

John: "They're always concerned about me wherever I go. When I take off on my bike they say 'Don't go too far, don't go too far.' They're always caring for me."

Carlos: "I think they love me because my Dad he works a lot and he works all day and even though he's tired he still plays ball with me outside."

Jody: "I know my parents love me because when I come home from school my parents always kiss me and hug me a lot and everything."

I KNOW SOMETHING'S WRONG AT HOME WHEN . . .

If you think Nixon was good at trying cover-ups, you should see some parents. They are absolutely convinced that they can keep their emotions hidden from their children. So, instead of dealing with stressful situations openly, they bury their problems and let them fester and grow, like a cavity. These parents are not fooling anyone. The kids know when something is wrong at home when:

69

Robbie: "You can just sense it around. Like if my mom and dad are mad at each other, you don't see the love around as much. They stop hugging each other."

Andy: "When I come home they always tell me how was my day at school. I know something's wrong if they, like, don't tell me that."

Bonnie: "They get angry at the children and they don't talk to each other, and they get angry at each other about things like my mom doesn't clean the house and my dad doesn't make the food right or something like that."

Christine: "I know something's wrong when they don't talk to each other. My dad usually works on the car and then my mom just goes into her bedroom and reads a book."

I KNOW EVERYTHING'S RIGHT AT HOME WHEN . . .

Just as kids know when something's wrong at home, they are wizards at understanding when everything is right. They happily pick up hints when:

Robin: "My parents are smiling and when they're real nice to each other and everybody else in the house. And then they take us out to eat."

Priscilla: "When my mom and dad are sitting on the bed with the bed vibrator on and watching TV and I'm outside playing with the dogs."

Rachel: "When they start laughing and telling jokes like the one about the monkey that drove the trailer truck."

Melanie: "When I come home from school, my mom opens the door and says, 'I had a great day, I went over to your grandfather's house and had some lunch.'"

Christie: "When sometimes my dad comes home and he'll tell us jokes the janitor told him."

Anna: "I knew things were good when I came home from school and my mom was putting whipped cream on her pumpkin pie and she squirted me in the face with it. That was the best."

WHAT PEOPLE COULD DO TO MAKE ME LESS LAZY

There are few parents in the known universe who have not muttered at some time, "Sure, I'd have plenty of time for romance if my kids were just not so lazy." This usually happens after mom or dad passes an empty hamper only to find a bathroom full of dirty size-six clothes.

Well, you can change the Tide of outrageous fortune

by following the suggestions these children offered:

Patrick: "1) Take away the computer (and computer games), 2) take away the TV set, 3) take away my football, 4) take away my bike, 5) threaten me with a bull whip, 6) give less time to do my work in, 7) take away the food, 8) let me play outside more, 9) don't give me work, 10) take away the telephone, 11) take away my friends, 12) let me sleep later, and 13) threaten me with a Samurai sword."

Kristina: "How my little sister can make me less lazy is stop singing 'She-Bop' and 'Girls Just Want to Have Fun.' So I can go to sleep at night. And another way to make my self less lazy is to throw cold water on my face in the morning."

Carlos: "By giving me more parties and less picking up poop."

John: "My parents could keep me from being lazy by not letting me do anything fun until I stop being lazy."

Jason: "My father could make me do Butterfly swimming stroke until my arms fall off and he could give me an IBM PC Jr."

Adam: "Pay me to work."

Jule: "If I was a parent I would, 1) Nag, 2) take things

away, 3) Go on strike—it's what my parents do to punish me and my sister. They don't do anything at all for us. NOTHING."

Jen: "Treat me to an ice cream every time I finish."

THE BEST GIFT OF LOVE IN THE WHOLE WORLD IS . . .

Take a good look at your child. You know, that freckle-faced mass of peanut butter-plasm who strafes you with Go-bots and plans on becoming a Master of the Universe. How much do you think he or she knows about your romance? About your problems? About your fondest desires?

Ask the kid. Or ask what he or she would wish for you. You're likely to be amazed with answers like:

Andrew: "I wish for my mother a couple of things/ A brand new car, a diamond ring/ Her very own army, that's not all/ A gigantic palace surrounded with walls/ A thousand servants that kneel at her feet/ The solar system would be quite a treat/ A yacht so she will not drown/ And happiness so she will not frown."

Ricky: "I would like my mother and father to get a free trip to New York and three million dollars to spend on the most expensive restraunt in town. I'd get brother a lifetime supply of ice cream (the kid likes it). For my two grandmas (great grandma and grandma) I'd give them a 100,000 dollars each in QUARTERS to go to

Las Vegas and last but not least my grandpa I'd get 800 miles of biking path to himself."

Colleen: "My wishes are that my Dad be healthier. I wish this because he has had polymyositis for 3 years. Mom; My wishes for my Mom are that she have everything she wants. I wish this because my dad gets mad at her sometimes."

Kendra: "I wish that my mom would have a free certificate to go into a antique shop and get everything that she likes because of that certificate and yet still get to keep the certificate. I also wish that my mom could win a trip to Europe by going on 'Wheel of Fortune' because she's good at playing it."

Richard: "I'd like to see my father marry my mother again, because they are divorsed. I'd like to see my mother have a good time with dad if they don't get married again, because I don't like it when they get mad at each other. I'd like my mom to get a new saw, and last night I accidently burned my mom's plastic bowl and because I rusted my mom's saw. I'd like to get my dad a new shirt, because that is all we can find him."

Seth: "I wish my mom could get a $100,000,000.00 because we are so poor because my dad will not give us child suport checks. I wish my dad had a $41,000.99 limosine so we could ride around and give people rides so he could become rich. I wish grandmother would go to Parise so she could bring back what good food they have."

Leshar: "My wish for my mom is for her to go to Paris because she deserves a month of and enjoy herself. My wish for my dad is that he can be happy and stop smoking. Because my dad deserves to be happy and not lonely. I don't want him to get lung cancer."

Dylan: "I wish my Mother had a diamond necklace that she saw in her favorite magazine, it costs $240,000 and I wish she had this because it would cheer her up after her long day of work."

Jason: "Mom—$90,000,000 because she needs it and a maid and to have her VA back because she can't bye a house. Granny—her land paid off and have 4,000,000. Papa—owns a big lake because he likes to fish. Grandma—more animals because she takes good care of them. Dad—to own the Dallas Cowboys because he likes them."

Lars: "I think my mother needs to have a collection of mint condition original records. Especially Elvis."

Aaron: "The best gift of love I could give would be to my mother. It would be a city for her to live in where everyone was a friend. That way, people could walk

anywhere, anytime without having to worry about being robbed or kidnapped."

THE MOST IMPORTANT THING
IN THE WORLD TO MY PARENTS IS . . .

How well-adjusted are you? Would you sell your soul
to nibble a wedge of brie with Barry Manilow? Would
you stand fast and faithful even if offered a hot tub full of
the Dallas Cowboy cheerleaders? Your children know
the most important things in the world to their parents,
and more:

Andy: "My brother and my sister and me. I can tell
because they hug us and they kiss us and stuff."

Jennifer: "Me. Because they take care of us and
brought us into life."

Melanie: "Both of them. And their whole house and
how the yard is taken care of. The really like each other
and one time, I'll make a long story short, one time my
father went to Montana and they were apart for like
three months and then they knew that they liked each
other more than that so they never go apart now."

Raul: "Their car and truck because they fix it all the
time. They spend lots of time with me, too. I'm worth
it."

Tim: "Each other. Because they care about each other and they help each other through hard times and everything. My mom told me this story about, when she was just getting out of college, she ran out of money and she couldn't stay in her dorm anymore and my Dad he loaned her the money to get her through. And she did."

MY PARENTS SHOULD GET AWAY FOR ROMANCE TO . . .

Sometimes you just have to get away from it all. And we're not talking about spending an afternoon reading the *Reader's Digest* in the bathroom, either. We're talking about the ultimate romantic vacation. We're talking about that one trip that exists only in the dreams of your children:

Jule: "I would send my parents first to Switzerland. At the Switz airport there waiting for them would be a limousene with the *works*. It would have a bed and TV in it. Also some chilled champane and caviar. The limousene would take them to the best Switz hotel there is for two weeks. A private jet would take them to Hong Kong, China. At the airport some enemie spys would follow them to their hotel, kidnap them and hold them ransom for the famous samerie sword of Hong Kong. (Be cool, I'm just kidding.) After that, since I would be broke, I would send for them in a dumpy old jeep and have a regular old life (Thank God)."

Adam: "My parents would go to lake Taho. They would stay at the most expensive and romantic hotel in the area. The hotel would have ten overhead fans in the restaurant area. And it would have two in each hotel room. Every day they would go out on the lake in a private canoe and anchor out somewhere in the middle of the lake and smooch for a couple of hours."

Felicia: "I would send my parents on a fourteen day cruise to Paris when they got there they would stay in the best hotel in Paris for one week then come back on another fourteen day cruise by then mom would have forgotten how bratty my brother and I are."

Doug: "First they'd take a caribbean cruise to Australia and spend fourteen days in a secluded camp surrounded by a lake with waiters and waitresses to serve their every command. Then they would sail to Ireland and would stay there for a week. Then they'd go back to Iowa on a plane and stay with my grandparents for four days."

David: "I would send my parents all around the world trip on a plane. And my parents will have so many souveniers that they will need a moving van to carry them home."

How I Show Someone I Love Them

How did you learn about love? Chances are you

learned about love from your parents. And—even as you read this—your offspring are learning about love from you.

Knowing that children learn what they live, I was interested in discovering how they would say they showed their love. Were their parents doing a good job? Or were today's future lovers destined to become duds? Relax, moms and dads. Your children will do just fine:

Jeffrey: "I show my love by encouraging my brother not to give up. And treating my parents to ice cream. Helping my mother do dishes clean the furniture and fix dinner."

Richard: "I give love to my mom when I help her around the house. I give love to my dad by helping him with breakfasts on Sundays. I give love to my sister by playing He-Man with her."

Colleen: "I show my love to my mother by getting her breakfast in bed. She knows I love her when I do this because I wouldn't do this if I didn't love her."

Elisenda: "I show my love to my mom by smiling and being in a good mood, because she's always telling me to smile and not be in a bad mood. I show my love to my father by helping him with the housework because our house is always such a mess!"

Ricky: "I show my love to my girlfriend by giving her

a nice big smile when she's happy or tell her a joke to cheer her up when she's sad."

Erin: "I show my love to my mom and dad by helping with the house work and cooking and loading the dishwasher. The way I show my love to my sister is by leaving her alone for the rest of her life."

Damon: "I show my love by not being mean and cruel to others. By doing things around the house. Once I cleaned and vacuumed all of the living room for mom while she was taking a nap."

Kendra: "I show my love by hugging. I also show my love by holding hands with my mom, another way I show my love is I get her a coke while she's ironing or getting her afghan when she's cold. My favorite thing to do to show my love is to snuggle her."

Tom: "I show my love by helping my mother put up the dishes every night and lending her money when she needs it. I also made my mother breakfast one morning and she just loved it. But my favorite way of showing people my love is putting my arms around them and saying 'I love you.'"

Andrew: "I show my love to my mother by being her slave. I show my love to my father by doing whatever he says also. I show my love to my sister by not killing her every time she is rude to me. I show my love to my dog by feeding him and giving him water most of the time."

Aaron: "I show my love for certain people by going out of my way to be nice to them. Like petting my dog, or washing the dishes, or even watching 'Sesame Street' with my little brother."

Nathan: "I show my love by helping my mom with house work, I show my love to my pets by feeding them and peting them, I show my love to my brother and friends by playing games with them, and I show my love to my dad by helping him with work. Love is very nice and sweet."

THE MEANING OF LOVE IS . . .

What is love? I wonder how many wise men and women have struggled with this question? Well, at least you can stop struggling. These kids—unburdened by adult neuroses—knew the answers in an instant. What is love? Just ask:

Craig: "The meaning of love is when I don't clober my brother as much as I do. When I wash the dishes for my mother. When I take the grabage out to the streets for my dad. When I go to bed with out my parents telling me to."

Simoni: "I think love is when I snuggle with my dog Hershy, and when people will care for the poor. Love is when friends get together and don't fight like Beth, Tracy, and Dena, all of us never fight with each other. The best thing is helping people like your mom and your family. Love is when teachers are nice like Mrs. Leon. Love is in your heart but you have to find it."

Dena: "The feeling of love is sweet and soft. I show my love to my mom and dad by cleaning the yard, doing house work. I also show love by being, and my family shows love to me for being there for me. I show my love for my teacher by being at school. Love feels so sweet, but can be sour."

Tanya: "The meaning of love is caring for each other. I show my love by comforting people that in the blue, and I like to let them know their somebody."

Marshanda: "Love is when you do nice things for your mom and dad. Love is when you cook dinner. Love is when you is helping someone when the person is very hert. Love is when you let you friends come for your birthday party."

Rowena: "Showing your love is by caring for others. Showing your love is by bunches of kisses and thousands of hugs. Showing your love is by helping your mother with the loundry. And helping your brother by helping him pick up his toys. I think showing your love is great don't you."

Thomas: "Love is giving presents to your friends presents at their birthday. Love is giving a hug to your mother and father. Love is not teling the cook at school that her food is terribul. Love is watching *Friday the 13th* with your father. Love is very nice."

Matt: "Love means sharing my toys with my brothers and sisters. Love means changing your hamsters cage. Love means giving my friends computer disks."

Katie: "To me love means sharing things, freind ship and nice people smiling to each other. also I think love is understanding something and singing and winning a spelling contist."

Jeff: "What love means to me is when I pull off my fathers shoes when hes had a hard day at work and in the morning I wake up on time for my mom. And when my father helps me with my computer."

Reggie: "Love means to me as a big sloppy kiss from your dog. A hug and kiss or even a pat on the head shows love."

Dawn: "I think love means caring for parents, sharing with other people, hugging soft teddy bears, doing chores, making dinner, and most of all, not to be a little stinker while mom is shopping."

I couldn't have said it better myself.

Ladies—There Are Cures for the Common Clydesdales

"Clod." "Klutz." "Clydesdale." Who are we talking about here? a) Tom Selleck, b) Mother Teresa, c) Typical American Husband or d) None of the above. Your answer please.

Time's up. You are absolutely and undeniably wrong—completely and massively incorrect—unless you picked d) None of the above. That's right, *none* of the above. Obviously, Tom and Mom don't fit the description. But, as you will soon discover, neither do America's hapless hubbies.

"But Langdon, amigo, that's not what I've been led to believe," you gasp in reply. No joke. And I think it's about time we took a good look at exactly who has led you to believe otherwise. These well-meaning folks are the reason why:

AMERICA IS MYTHING OUT ON ROMANCE

Now, no one person is responsible for convincing us that all husbands are jerks. But some people aren't helping things much, either. People like Ann Landers and other expert advisers.

Ann Landers and America's assorted amorous experts have the same job. They exist to give helpful advice to people who desperately need it. And most of the people with advice to give are desperately good at it. But their consistent theme of helping the helpless may myth-lead people into believing that most folks are losers. And especially that most folks are losers in the land of love.

Take Ann's 1985 survey on sex, for example. After tallying up the responses, she concluded that the majority of wives would rather do most anything than make love to their husbands. Obviously, the women she heard from were unhappy. But when was the last time you heard anyone say, "Gee, I'm so happy I think I'll write Ann Landers."

Intelligent and perceptive reader, there *are* lots of happy wives out there. They are happy to be married to some of America's good guys. They are thrilled to know the passion of unbelievably good love. And I think you'll be thrilled to finally hear from them.

Why do I make such an emotional judgment? Because these are men who are good at what they do. You don't learn tennis from a schlep who hits every other ball into the net. You don't take singing lessons from a woman who has been sued by the Society for the Prevention of Cruelty to Neighbors. And you don't learn how to be a truly romantic and masculine lover from a guy who is a charter member of the Geek of the Month Club.

The men described in the following letters are some of America's Good Guys. They are good husbands, good fathers and great lovers. They are what every man can and should be.

If you want to be a Good Guy, or if you want your partner to be one, take note. Make a list of those qualities you find particularly attractive. Remember that imitation is the sincerest form of flattery. And it's about time that America's women were sincerely flattered.

We start by asking that passionate question:

WHAT IS A GOOD GUY?
by Melodee Tomsu

A good guy is a husband who still opens your car door after ten years of marriage.

A good guy is a husband who is very nice to relatives he doesn't especially like.

A good guy is a husband who sweeps, dusts, cleans bathrooms, washes dishes, and does laundry as much as I do.

A good guy is a husband who takes his overweight

wife out on a bike ride and coaxes her to make that one last mile while never once complaining about her weight in ten years of marriage.

A good guy is a husband who doesn't need special occasions to surprise me with dinner or a rose.

A good guy is a husband who still enjoys teasing and playing practical jokes on his wife.

A good guy is a husband who will wake up at 5:30 AM to go bird watching with his wife.

A good guy is a husband who doesn't rant and rave at you when you break the lawn mower.

A good guy is a husband who supports your decision to quit your job even though your combined income level drops by 40%.

A good guy is a husband who after ten years of marriage comes home early from work because he missed you and wanted to be with you.

This good guy is my adoring husband who puts me on a ten-foot pedestal a hundred times a day. If just plain being nice could be packaged and sold, then my husband and I would be millionaires. ♡

Did you catch Melodee's very valuable phrase? It's "just plain being nice." Far too many men are uncaring and uncouth. In fact, their idea of a "stable" relationship is acting like a sex jockey and leaving your house looking like a barn. But there is a cure.

For wives, it begins by asking yourself a very personal question: "Did I marry an idiot? Did I pick a man who thinks people from Tobago are called Toboggans?" Of course you didn't. Your man—though he may occasionally eat, drink, talk and smell like a Clydesdale— has his good points. And to help those good points shine through, you can polish his romance by following these three easy secrets:

1) Show him what a husband or partner is supposed to be.

Frankly, many guys have never knowingly seen or met a "good" husband. (It's not that they are rare. They just don't advertise.) And if you think that's a little scary, then you'll be petrified to learn that men, almost without exception, learn about husbanding from their dear old Dads. Think about that. Would you like to spend the rest of your life married to the spitting image of your father-in-law? I didn't think so.

You can keep this from happening—and you can protect your sons in the bargain—by showing your man what a husband or partner is *supposed* to be. You can show him, discreetly of course, the stories of marvelous manhood in this chapter. Once you've done that, then you can gallop on over to . . .

2) Tell him that this is the kind of man you would do anything for, anytime and anywhere.

Why should your man strive to be one of America's good guys? Because you'll love him forever. Because you'll willingly play pirate and captive. Because you will, in turn, strive to become one of America's "good" women. Like I said, guys know a good thing when they see it. It's time you showed him your good thing, too.

3) Praise his every, and any, effort at romance.

You and I know that you're not going to cure your Clydesdale overnight. (What fun would that be, anyway?) It's going to take time, and it's going to take your loving praises: "A lube gun for my Honda? Ralph, what a thoughtful gesture." Or even, "You made me breakfast in bed? Oh darling, I've never had Wheaties flambé before." Praise your partner's every effort at romance. And then watch your burning passion grow.

If you do this, I guarantee (well, almost) that you'll soon cuddle with your partner and breathily whisper in his ear, "Snookums, you are:"

MY MAN OF A MAN
by Mrs. Darryl Thomas

I have been married to the most loving man in the world for 20 years—the greatest years of my life. We have four teenagers in the house and they are always teasing us about being so huggy-kissy. Yes, we have kept romance in our lives. But, with a husband like mine, it is so easy.

He sends me flowers for no occasion, and for all occasions. But with us both working, what I like most about my hubby is the way he helps me around the house so that we can spend more time together. I have to be to work by 7:00 a.m., so this leaves him to get the kids off to school by himself. By the time the kids are off, he has the breakfast dishes done, a load of wash in, all the beds made, and the house all picked up, so that when I come home from work all I have to do is fix dinner. Together we clean up afterwards.

This makes for a more cozy evening and leaves more time for romance that otherwise we would be too tired for. He has always cared for how I feel when making love, not just himself. He is just the greatest lover around, gentle with a "slow hand." He is always leaving love notes all over the house; on mirrors, on my pillow, in my dresser drawers, you name it.

My guy may sound like a wimp, but he's certainly *not*. He's a good looking construction worker. Romance is not dead in the good old USA. ♡

Yesirree Bob—and the rest of you guys out there— women want a man who is *strong* enough to care. They also want:

A SPECIAL, SPECIAL MAN
by Mrs. David Wheeler

We were newlyweds (second time for me) when I decided to prepare my new husband his favorite food for dinner. The day was hectic with three small children. The evening started even worse.

We had no extra money for babysitters and time

alone was rare. Everything went wrong. The kids were fed early and put to bed. Put to bed *many* times, in fact. So many times that my hope of having a nice, quiet, romantic evening was waning fast.

To make things worse yet, my husband was ten minutes later than usual and by the time he arrived my carefully planned meal was burned and I was in tears. He held me tenderly while I sobbed out my story finishing with " . . . and, and, I wanted it to be so *special* for you."

He listened to it all then quietly said, "It *is* special—you don't burn dinner *every* night."

With a sense of humor, love and understanding like that, is it any wonder I've kept my wonderful romantic man for over 25 years? ♡

It's also no wonder that women want a man who is soft, but not too mushy, when it comes to love. Men like Ben Duree. His wife, Daisy, wrote:

THE BIG CHEESE OF MY LIFE
by Daisy Duree

Most women would not think of my husband as the World's Greatest Lover. But to me he is that because he does things for me that are kind and considerate, not just at certain times or days, but on an everyday basis and from morning till night.

Like opening the garage door for me when he knows

it's about time for me to come home, or opening and closing the gate to our yard when I drive up so that I don't have to get out. Like having a surprise meal cooked for me when I come home from a hard day at work. My husband is 72 years young, and I work part-time, so I do appreciate his gestures. Nobody else would understand these gestures as love.

One incident that will stay in my mind always is when my husband went to California to see and visit his widowed mother. When he came back on the plane let me tell you what he had packed in his suitcase for me. Number One, he knows I love gardenias and I also love a special kind of cheese that is very hard to get here. It's called Liederkranz, a soft ripened cheese, that has quite an odor to it.

When he got his luggage from the baggage department and we got to the car, he opened his suitcase and packed in with his clothes he had a gardenia corsage in a nice container on one side of the suitcase and my special stinky cheese wrapped up in lots of foil and a brown paper bag in the other. I laughed and cried at the same time as I could still smell my cheese over everything. But I was very touched by his gesture of love and his effort to bring this to me intact.

He is not a mushy man, but shows his love in little ways like that. Yet he is 100% man by taking care of all our needs here on the ranch, with repairs and the cattle and our water problems with our well. I depend on him and need him, for without his little love gestures, my life would be very empty. P.S. His pet name for me is Fluffy. ♡

By now, you're probably asking yourself, "Where in heaven did Langdon find these guys—at Sammy Spiegel's Center for Sainthood?" Heck, no. These men are everywhere. They are your neighbors, your co-workers and your friends. And they thrive wherever women are willing to urge them on.

That's an important point that I don't want you to miss. It's not just that these guys are good; it's that their wives or partners are happy to tell them they're good. This positive reinforcement is the *single* most impor-tant secret in making your man more romantic.

Look at it this way: If a child grows up being told he is stupid, then, even if he's a potential genius, he is sure to feel stupid. And if a husband is told that he is "un-romantic," then, even if he is a budding Casanova, he is sure to become a common Clydesdale. A warm-hearted winner or a limpid loser? Ladies, the choice is yours.

Use the power of positive passion. Tell your partner that he's a good guy. And try to understand:

HIS QUASI-MOTIVES OF LOVE
by Connie Jo Pratt

The house is quiet; it pops and snaps as the evening grows cooler. I sit alone in our home, remembering the past 14 years. A question comes to mind, "Is he one of the most romantic men around?" My first, silent answer would be . . . probably not . . . if romance is receiving flowers, "off-the-wall" cards, private dinners for two or little unexpected gifts. Over the years I have received my share of the above, with great surprise, joy and wonderment; however, that doesn't make him "Casanova Jim."

On the other hand, if romance is being patient when he wants to talk and I'm too busy with the kids to listen. If being romantic is coming out of the bathroom dressed like the Hunchback of Notre Dame and making me laugh when I'm so angry at him I could poke out his eyeballs. If being romantic is him quietly rummaging through drawers and closets in search of an item I threw out weeks ago.

If being romantic is smooching in the kitchen while I give a tired child a spelling test for the fifth time and he yells at the other child to turn down the radio. If being romantic is him making me feel content, secure and loved while sitting alone in our living room waiting for him to come home from work, then he *is* the most romantic man in the world. ♡

Let's take a break here, guys. I want you to lean back and mull these stories over. I want you to ruminate in your recliners by asking yourself, "What do these men give that I don't?" The answer isn't just "more thought," "more time" or "more bucks."

The only thing that uniquely distinguishes these

good guys is that they give a damn. They care enough to do *something,* anything that says "I care." And friends, it doesn't have to be much:

- ♥ A hand squeeze while watching TV.
- ♥ A hot cup of coffee brought to bed in the morning.
- ♥ Or a diaper changed even when it's not your turn.

Andy Schneider, for example, won the heart of his woman with surprisingly little rhyme or reason. His fiancée called their story:

ROSES ARE RED & I'M NOT BLUE
by Marcy Saims

Andy is a lot of things to me. He's the one who didn't get angry when I drove over a bucket of oil in his garage spreading dirty oil all over the floor. He was there to hold me when I ate too many double-stuffed Oreos and ended up, literally, spilling my cookies. He's the guy who mistakenly uttered "I love you" for the first time at the airport. (His head wasn't prepared for what his heart was saying.) He's the animal lover who found a gila monster roaming around his yard and returned it to the desert to be with its friends.

He's the "shy guy turned cutie pie" who, four years later, still composes original verses such as this recently acquired ditty: "Roses are red/ Violets are blue/ But you're still #1/ In my book." He's Andy Schneider. My main man, my main squeeze, my future husband. ♡

Let's see. Women want a man who is *strong* enough

to care, *soft* but not too mushy, *fun-loving* (you know, guys who play their hunches) and *upbeat* when things are at their worst (or should I say versed). What more could they ask for? How about a man who is:

A FAN OF HIS FAMILY
by Brenda Pennington

Oh, what gratitude to have the opportunity to expound on the virtues of Dean Pennington. Dean is my romantic husband. Over the past 20 years his love has manifested itself in many unusual ways. What better way to keep the love light shining than to awaken in the morning to a message of a scavenger hunt for Christmas presents? Toilet-paper notes taped to the ceiling of the kitchen. "Have a good day honey, I love you" love letters rolled up in the toilet paper roll. Even after 20 years I still receive love notes written on the bathroom mirror when I get up in the morning. (He didn't want to wake me at 5 a.m. to tell me to have a good day and that he loves me.)

His life is lived for us. When I went to work, he pitched in with the housework. That was great, but he saw I was having a time keeping up the laundry and the ironing, so he took over the shirts and blouses while I did the slacks and skirts. When my day has gone down the tubes, he cooks dinner. What wife could not feel romantic about a man who has just cooked dinner and then cleaned the kitchen?

Let me tell you one more thing. I had talked for the

last year about putting in ceiling fans in our house when we moved back West. When we arrived, he went out and purchased the fans and installed them. This might not seem like such a big deal, except the temperature outside was above 100 degrees, and the attic was unbearable. He insisted that he put them in before he left on a business trip because he wanted the kids and me to have the use of the fans while he was gone. I thank the Lord for my husband for he is truly America's Best Good Guy. ♡

American women are also fans of:

A SEDUCTIVE LIFELONG LOVER
by Doris Faulkner

We older couples still treasure fond memories of the excitement and passion of some of the "new" ideas expressed in Romance! You might be surprised at the many innovations we were able to dream up to keep the romance in our marriage alive.

My husband is 76 and I am going on 74 and although there is snow on the roof, the fire in the furnace still glows, and occasionally it will burst into a brief but intense flame which is even more precious because it is no longer commonplace.

Through our 54 years of marriage we have experienced many joys, a few sorrows, some triumphs and some disappointments, but with each experience our love has grown and through trial and error we have learned that *communication* is the most important aspect of a true relationship. If anything were to happen to me, he would have no reason to sigh, "If only I had told her more often how much I loved her."

The years have rolled swiftly by, but I still carry the image in my heart of the way he looked as he stood waiting for me as I walked down that long church aisle nearly 54 years ago. He still is the handsomest man I know and I tell him how proud I am of him every time we go out together.

I guess true love really is blind, for I am old and wrinkled; there are silver threads among the gold, and I bulge and sag in all the wrong places, but only last week as we were preparing for bed he remarked, "Honey you have no idea how seductive you look in that nightie." ♡

In addition to a man who unsaggingly loves his wife, women want a man who can truly be called:

THE WORLD'S GREATEST LOVER
by Jeanette Wright

In my opinion, my husband is the greatest. He always gets up first, plugs in the coffee and then comes and says, "It's a beautiful day. I love you, sweetheart." He always remembers our anniversaries, birthdays and even makes up special days for us to go out and dine together.

But he is a lover of more than just his wife and children. He has a sense of caring and love for people everywhere. When there was a drought in the Sahel in Africa, he—at his own expense—went to the university and secured 21 varieties of wheat to be planted in seed plots to provide new and stronger strains of this valuable grain. He did this in two weeks on his vacation time. People today plant their fields in this new grain.

He did the same in Central America. He paid his own way to Costa Rica and took new adapted varieties of wheat and triticale to the poorest people in that country.

More recently, my husband saw the problems of drug abuse among our youth here in town. He studied the problem and decided to go as a volunteer to Southeast Asia to try and introduce new crops as substitutes for opium poppy. He worked with the United Nations program for drug abuse and spent a year persuading the Hill Tribe people of Thailand, Laos and Burma to grow beans and coffee. Reports came back that the heroin export of that area dropped from 90 tons to 50 tons in the crops that followed.

Today, he still thinks about what he can do. At present he gathers clothes and food from churches in this area and trucks them to the needy in Mexico. I guess I call him a great lover because he fulfills the words of someone who once said, "Greater love has no man than this, that a man give his life for others." ♡

OK, OK, so Jeanette's husband really is a saint. Other men can still qualify as the World's Greatest Lover by making a sincere—and significant—sacrifice. Take a guy like Brian J. Perona. His wife, Jane, wrote:

HE MAKES MY WHOLE WORLD SING
by Jane Perona

I have been married to the World's Greatest Lover for almost six years. We are also expecting our first baby, who is due to arrive any day. When I was in my fourth month of pregnancy, my appetite was ravenous. I woke up one night at 12:30 a.m. craving a Burger King Whopper with *everything.* I sat up in bed, turned on the light and considered trying to forget my craving when Brian woke up and said, "You're hungry, aren't you? What can I get you?" When I told him what I was craving, he got out of bed, got dressed, found his keys and went out searching for a late-night Burger King Drive-Thru. He found one.

Brian risks rush-hour traffic every Friday afternoon to go to a flower shop and bring me home a bunch of daisies because he knows they're my favorite flower. My Greatest Lover has learned all the words to the old Barry Manilow songs so that he can sing along with me when the tape is in our car tape deck. He does this so I don't feel silly singing by myself. He even surprised me with tickets to Barry's recent concert. I failed to mention that Brian is a rock and roll fan and *hates* Barry Manilow. But he does this because he loves me.

Brian will fight my battles for me. The battles that I seem to have with spiders and bugs. If he sees one that I don't, he'll avert my attention and quietly kill it. And my World's Greatest Lover will challenge me to a wicked game of Scrabble, carry an overwhelming lead, but help me use my Q or X tile before he wins. All of this he does, because he loves me. ♡

Yes friend, Barry Manilow—the ultimate test of love. Unless, of course, you're tested by:

A WAISTED SECOND HONEYMOON?
by Cheryl Paige

When my husband and I celebrated our 10th wedding anniversary last month, I was nine months pregnant. We had promised ourselves, the day of our wedding, that on our 10th anniversary we would share a second honeymoon. My husband didn't let my enlarged waistline and 35 extra pounds stop us.

He arranged care for our other children for the weekend, and checked us into a suite in a local hotel. He sent me flowers (an arrangement of the same flowers I carried in our wedding), purchased non-alcoholic champagne (because of my condition), and spent the three days wining and dining me. I've never felt more like a queen. P.S. Two weeks to the day after our romantic weekend, our baby was born, Emily Anne. (He's a wonderful dad, too.) ♡

And literally putting romance to the test was one woman who faced:

A FINAL FAILURE—BUT NOT OF LOVE
by Doreen Joffee

I know that Alex is thinking of me all the time, not only by his words and actions, but by how attuned he is to me even over hundreds of miles. Shortly before we were married, school took me to another state for a year. That was an incredibly difficult time for me and, even though our phone bills were enormous, how could Alex know just when I was feeling the absolute lowest? For on those few occasions, when I was heading home for a good cry, a beautiful bouquet of flowers would head me off at my door and greet me.

Now that we are married the romance hasn't ended. We don't have much money so we stay home most evenings, but Alex makes them as special as if we were going out on the town. Last week he planned a romantic evening for us and let me know only that, so I could share in the joy of anticipation. When I got home there was a single red rose, a chocolate kiss and a note on the door telling me to come on in but keep my "pretty brown eyes" closed.

When I entered, and he told me to take a peek, I could see why he had me shut my eyes. Our living/dining room had been so transformed it must have taken hours. He had cleaned the entire apartment and had placed candles all around which were glowing almost as much as my wonderful husband. We ate and then spent the rest of the evening slow dancing by the glow of the candles.

My husband certainly is the romantic mover in the family, but I think one other illustration will show that his consideration for me knows no bounds. Two summers ago we had planned a splurge trip through Europe to visit many friends and relatives. Due to his schedule, this was his last chance for many years to get that amount of time off. He had also worked hard that year and really needed the vacation. Unfortunately, shortly before we were to leave, I found out that I'd failed a final and the only way I could continue the next year would be to take the course over that summer. I was devastated.

There was no choice for me, but I asked him to go without me, assuring him I wouldn't mind. Alex wouldn't hear of it. He spent his summer off caring for me—cooking, cleaning, doing laundry—freeing me from anything which would hinder my studies. He *never* mentioned Europe or blamed me for our not going. In fact, at the end of my course, we were able to get away for ten days and explore the country on a camping trip he arranged. ♡

Gosh these guys are good. And their message is good too. To men it goes something like: "Give a damn and get a lot in return." And to women it says, "Your man is exactly as good as you believe him to be."

Give a little extra effort. Think good thoughts. And

load your notebook with great tips as you read the final Good Guy stories. We begin with:

BOUNCING BABY BOOMER BUMPERS
by Betsy Bradshaw

For months I have been forming this letter in my mind. My husband Bob is so special that it has been hard to pick only one or two romantic events. Just last week he sneaked a half-dozen gooey chocolate donuts past our three children for a midnight snack. I had mentioned a silly craving for chocolate. Believe me, it is no easy task to slip something like chocolate past our children.

There are two events that probably best illustrate the strength, compassion and romance of this man. There was the Saturday afternoon he showed up with a solitaire diamond. I was hot, grumpy and rushing around trying to clean the house for a party the next day. We had two children at the time. Bob slipped out and returned a couple of hours later with this sweet and simple ring that forever sparkles. He told me he felt that I should have a diamond because I would look good in them. We had been married seven years at the time.

Last December we had our third baby. We practiced our Lamaze technique and he listened to me night after night in preparation for our baby. However, it turned out the birth was more sudden than we expected. When it became apparent that we would not make the hospital in time, he delivered our second son in our van. He got help afterwards and virtually took over my care at the hospital. His tenderness, level head and sense of humor turned what could have been a traumatic event into one that I remember as being safe, secure and completely unorthodox.

Like all people in love, I really cannot express how it feels to be the partner of someone this special. I feel as if each day has a pot of gold at the end. We have been together nine years and worked hard for the things we have. Because of Bob I have an attitude of faith and love which makes my life and the lives of our children glow. I love you Bob. ♡

(Just a quick Mr. Romance Note: In honor of the baby's birthplace, Bob and Betsy named their child Thomas "Bumpers" Bradshaw.)

HE RUBS ME THE RIGHT WAY
by Terry Hawes

My Mr. Good Guy will get up at 5:00 a.m. and feed our baby. When I come home from work, he will massage my feet and back (I'm a cashier and stand a lot) without me even asking him to—and even after he's had just as hard of a day. He knows the right time to come up and give me a hug so I won't go crazy. It somehow eases all the tension out of you. He'll tell the kids as I'm making popcorn or reading them a book, "We're so lucky to have a mom like our mommy. She loves us so much."

When we go camping, he'll roast my marshmallows over the campfire for me because mine always burn. He plans romantic evenings out without the kids and some really beautiful weekends. I'll come home and our stuff will be packed, the kids are ready to go to grandma's and when we get to our destination (usually the ocean), we'll walk into a nice room with a view and there will already be a bottle of champagne on the table or a rose in a vase. I really don't know how or why I ever got so lucky to find such a caring, gentle man and after nine years of marriage and two kids no less. ♡

THERE'S A LOTTA LOVE IN THE LOVE LOTTO
by Diane Vasko

I met my husband Mickey 20 years ago on April 1st, but I have not been fooled one bit during the 18 years we have been married. He was and still is a very kind, loving, and thoughtful man. We are blessed with three wonderful children who are indeed lucky to have such a patient (most of the time) and caring Dad.

Mick has a special way of making everyday living more than just routine—the cards he sends for no special reason, the frequent invitations to meet him for lunch, the daffodils on a bright spring day, the roadside bouquets in summer, satisfying my sweet tooth with Snickers candy bars, and making time just for us.

On our 15th anniversary, we had a first *real* get-away vacation from the children. I noticed this rather old, dusty brown box that the busboy was carrying into the hotel room. Here were all of our souvenirs of dating, our wedding and honeymoon pictures, and special cards we had kept over the years. What fun we had reminiscing with both laughter and tears.

Last February I seemed to be entering any and every sweepstakes contest. One day I received a telegram in the mail and thinking it was just another sweepstakes entry, I almost threw it away. Here Mick had sent this notice that I won the You-Deserve-A-Break Sweepstakes. He made all the arrangements at a lovely motel resort, the children were taken care of, and we were off for a romantic weekend. What a surprise. Mick and I know that ours is forever an "April Love." ♡

21 YEARS OF LOVE WITH THE JAVA MAN
by Beverly Franklin

My husband wakes me every morning by bringing a hot cup of coffee. And it's always delivered with a good-morning kiss. He's been doing this since our wedding day, 21 years ago. This may not seem so special, but it is, as he has never cared for coffee and never drinks it himself. He doesn't even care for the way it smells. It's the "little things" that mean so much. ♡

And, last of this happy handful is:

LOVE IS A WARM PISTON
by Lucille Montgomery

My husband and I had been married for 15 years, and

I had recently returned to work as a teller in a busy bank that stayed open until 7:30 p.m. on Fridays. It was a cold February day with a lot of snow on the ground, and I was unusually tired after a long, pressure-filled day. At the stroke of closing time I received a telephone call from my husband saying he would pick me up at 8 p.m. When I thanked him but reminded him that my car was sitting in the parking lot, he said, "I know it is, but you can drive my warm car home and I'll take yours." He had to drive 10 miles to perform this beautiful act of love. ♡

Lucille pegged it right, folks. Her good guy performed a simple, but beautiful, "act of love." It's how we all want to be treated. And it's how every one of us can—and should—live. All it takes is that little extra step. And, if your Good Guy quotient has room for just one more story, all it requires is:

A KISS, A CUDDLE AND A CARE
by Linda Carlson

When my husband and I were first married, I worked all night and he worked all day, leaving us only three hours to spend together. One morning when I came home from work, I was so exhausted that when my husband tried to "cuddle" a little before he went to work, I fell asleep in his arms. Needless to say, I felt awful when I awoke and found him gone—until I went into the bathroom and saw that my husband had washed the uniform I wore that night—by hand—and had hung it to dry. A note attached to it read: "I love you. Sorry you have to work so hard to help out. Thanks." We have been married 10 years and to this day he is just as romantic. ♡

Like I said, these guys—and your guy—are *good*. All you have to do is:

1) Show him what a husband or partner is supposed to be.
("A good guy is a husband who doesn't need special occasions to surprise me with dinner or a rose. A good guy is a husband who sweeps, dusts, cleans bathrooms, washes dishes and does laundry as much as I do." Melodee Tomsu)

2) Tell him that this is the kind of man you would do anything for, anytime and anywhere.
("I feel as if each day has a pot of gold at the end. Because of Bob I have an attitude of faith and love which makes my life and the lives of our children glow." Betsy Bradshaw)

3) Praise his every, and any, effort at romance.
("We have four teenagers in the house and they are always teasing us about being so huggy kissy. Yes, we have kept romance in our lives. But with a husband like mine, it is so easy." Mrs. Darryl Thomas)

Romance Makes the Stars Shine

OK, I have to admit it. So far I've been pretty tough on Hollywood types. I've called them hopeless hunk-ettes, style-less starlets and—can you believe it?—scheming studlets. I guess this means I'm *not* going to be invited to Joan Collins's house for chopped liver and crackers. Oh well, it's her paté and she can cry if she wants to.

I'm not going to. But I am going to tell you about a small galaxy of stars who have succeeded in the land of real-life love. Admittedly, it has taken several rehearsals for some, but right now each of the following folks has learned what it takes to be called one of America's Greatest Lovers.

It is exactly what you and I have learned so far—it's the little things that count.

Yes, their secret is out: Romance makes the stars shine. And they have never shined more brightly than in the following stories. We start with a few sterling thoughts from "Bonanza's Big Daddy":

Strumming Up Romance with His Ukelele
by Lorne Greene

Romance is the rose, the blush on your life. It's when you're walking around in a daze—and you say this can't be happening to me. Not because of a loved one necessarily, but because of things that are happening. And if they're nice things, it's romantic, if they're not nice things, oh my goodness, then it's the pits.

The most romantic thing that's happened to me was one particular incident when I was 18 years old. It was in 1933 while the Century of Progress exhibition was on in Chicago. My mother wanted to go to Chicago because we have relatives there. We stayed on with them for a month.

There was a gal that lived about two or three doors away, she was about my age, and we used to go down to the beach—it was summertime, of course—and I had a ukelele. I hate to admit it but I had a ukelele. We were, I think, very romantic. I would sing "Under a Blanket of Blue"—a great song in those days.

We were really a hot item for a while. But I left and went back to Canada and she went on to other things. Many years later my wife and I were in Florida. We were doing the Orange Bowl Parade, and there was a phone call one morning at the hotel. I answered the phone and this woman said, "Is this Mr. Lorne Greene?" and I said, "Yes, it is," and she said, "Well, my name is so and so, that shouldn't mean anything to you, but my mother is an old friend of yours."

I said "Really, who's your mother?" and she said, "Just a moment please, she's right here. She'd like to talk to you." So this woman comes on the phone singing "Under a Blanket of Blue." I fell down laughing. It was kind of nice, and it was kind of strange and kind of corny, but mostly it was kind of nice. ♡

Wow, Ben Cartwright riding the range with a ukelele. Wait until the folks at the Ponderosa hear about this. And speaking of the Ponderosa, don't forget about Michael Landon. Michael has eight, count 'em, eight children. In addition, he's known to millions as one of television's finest fathers, Pa Ingalls of "Little House on the Prairie." What's so surprising is that Michael, by his own admission, had far from perfect parents. In fact, their story could well be considered tragic. Here's what Michael said when I asked:

WERE YOUR PARENTS ROMANTIC?
by Michael Landon

My parents were not what you'd call romantic. In fact, they didn't care for each other at all. My father was

Jewish and my mother was Catholic. My father was not thrilled with Catholics, and my mother was very anti-Semitic. It didn't make for a great relationship. It was one of those families that has those wonderful six-week periods where they don't speak. They're eight feet apart and mother says, "Tell your father dinner's ready," and you say, "Dinner's ready." ♡

Obviously, TV's family man didn't learn the secrets of romantic passion from his parents. He was, however, able to overcome this obstacle through trial—and error—and love. (For you message buffs, remember the theme from Chapter 1: Love knows no obstacles, no barriers and has (thankfully) damn little common sense.)

Another man who has had his share of trials is the boss from "People's Court," the honorable Judge Wapner. He has a dreamily romantic story, too. The judge's great American romance began when his blind date smiled at him—and then fell asleep. Honestly. His sensationally sleepy story is called:

THE GIRL OF HIS DREAMS
by Judge Joseph Wapner

Certainly one of the most romantic moments with my wife, Mickey, was the first night we met. We had a blind date and we went to a dance. I was attracted to her but I don't think she was attracted to me. On the way home she fell asleep on my shoulder sitting there next to me. It was romantic, but it was not what we would call sexy.

Probably, *the* most romantic moment with Mickey was when she surprised me on my 50th birthday with a party.

That was nice. What she did was set up the party at some friends' house, in La Canada, which is quite a distance from where we live. She hired a bus. She told people to meet around the corner from our house in the bus and then she and I would go out, drive over to the bus, and then suddenly get on and everyone would yell surprise.

What happened was that one couple came by mistake straight to our door. Mickey answered it and I could hear her say, "No, no, no, it's over there, over there." So by that time, I knew something was going on, but I couldn't figure out exactly what it was. Then we left and went to the bus and there was the surprise. That was one of the nicest things she's ever done. It was a lot of fun. ♡

Also surprising is how a truly great love can grow from truly humble beginnings. Such was the case for this country's white-shoed King of Swoon:

THE BEST LOVE COMES IN THE SMALLEST PACKAGES
by Pat Boone

There have been many romantic moments in our life,

but I think the most romantic was our first Christmas— Shirley's and mine. When we moved to Texas, we had no money, we couldn't even buy Christmas gifts. Shirley got hold of a demo of a Christmas song I'd made with the Texas Boys Choir and wrapped it up and gave it to me for Christmas.

For her gift, I got three boxes, each one larger than the next, so she had to open three boxes. When she got down to the bottom of the smallest box, it was just a card in which I'd very carefully and lovingly written "I love you, Merry Christmas." That's all we had to give each other, but that's all we needed. I mean, that was a tender and romantic moment and it had nothing to do really with material things. It had to do with giving of ourselves and our deepest feelings to each other. ♡

Believe it or not, one of TV's greatest lovers failed when he tried to share his deepest feelings with his other. In fact, "General Hospital's" own Sean Donnelly (actor John Riley) can still remember being:

TONGUE-TIED & TERRIFIED
by John Riley

It was my first date. Oh Lord, I had to pick a girl up and take her to a movie. Of course, I didn't own a car, so we had to take a, a . . . bus. Not knowing what to say, and you're so much in love with this creature, you are *so* much in love. Her name was Yvonne, and she was blonde, and she was beautiful, and she was sweet and gorgeous and, oh, all of the things I, as a teenager, thought I wanted in a woman. And I just didn't know what to say. Conversation was at a minimum and it was like pulling teeth to get me to say anything. She was taking over most of the control to open me up and I was rather tongue-tied. I guess that's probably one of the most embarrassing things that's happened to me, because I had so much to say and it was all in my head, but my tongue wouldn't work. I was fifteen.

(Fortunately, John did get his tongue untied some years later when he had something very, very important to say.)

I proposed to my wife in a Mexican restaurant, and I hate Mexican food. And I said to my now wife, it's my second marriage, "If I ever thought of getting married again, it would be you," and she said, "Do you really mean that?" and I said "Yes, I do. I love you, will you marry me?" and she said, "Yes," and that was it.

It was very simple. I really didn't think about it, it was a natural result of the time we had spent with one another. It was a realization that hit me just sitting across the table from her, knowing that this woman would stop a bullet for me—and that I could stop a bullet for her. Anytime. Anywhere. ♡

I guess most people would have figured that the head hunk of "General Hospital" would have popped the question anytime and anywhere *except* while biting a burrito. The spicy truth is that stars have the same dreams, and the same meals, as the rest of us. If you find this hard to swallow, check out the following stories from three of John's daytime tube-mates. I asked Robyn Bernard (Terry Brock O'Connor on "General Hospital"), Tia Carrere (Jade on "General Hospital") and Holly Gagnier (Ivy on "Days of Our Lives") to describe their "most romantic moment." This, complete with ingredients, is what they said:

FRIED CHICKEN, BAKED BEANS & THOU
by Robyn Bernard

I like to go on picnics and things like that. The most romantic moment was when I went horseback riding in the Malibu mountains with my boyfriend at the time. We found a waterfall, just a little spot, and nobody was around. We couldn't see cars, couldn't see houses, it was really private.

I'd packed a lunch of fried chicken. I had cooked everything—fried chicken, corn on the cob, baked beans, french bread, cheese and a bottle of wine. I played music on a portable synthesizer. I played blues songs, Judy Garland songs, I played some of my songs that I wrote—oh yes, it was very, *very* romantic. ♡

HAPPINESS OFF THE HOOK
by Tia Carrere

I found it most romantic one evening when I was in

the kitchen puttering around with my sweetheart, just cooking dinner together, working together, no music, no television, no phone constantly ringing. It was very relaxed and romantic and we could take time out and talk to each other. That's it, but it was wonderful. ♡

SNUGGLING UP FOR LOVE
by Holly Gagnier

My most romantic moment was when I was in New York and it was freezing outside and it was midnight. My boyfriend and I took the Staten Island ferry so that we could see the New York skyline from the ferry. We just took it to Staten Island and took it right back. It was really romantic. We got hot chocolate and we stood out on the deck of the boat and froze to death, and just snuggled up with our chocolate and sat there under the stars. It was great. It was wonderful. ♡

"Wonderful" looks like it's the key word here. And so does the word "normal." Isn't it great to find out that Hollywood's heroes and heroines are just like us? They've discovered that love is found, not on camera, but in the little things that mean so much. In the love of a family, on the strings of a ukelele, in the smallest of gifts and in the most "ordinary" of moments.

Romance does make the stars shine. And—thank heaven—it can also make them laugh, as in these final thoughts from that passionately popular comedian, Will Shriner:

THE SPAWN OF ROMANCE
by Will Shriner

I'm married, my wife is pregnant—we think she's pregnant—we're keeping the rabbit on life-support systems right now. And love is terrific.

We were engaged for about five minutes. But it was a good five minutes. We lived together first, then we figured, what the heck, we need a blender, so we just went ahead and got married. Have a big wedding— that's the key if you're going to get married—because the gifts come rolling in. We got a Mr. Coffee for every room in our house.

My wife and I also have a very normal sex life. She dresses up in a trout suit and we spawn. But seriously, romance is something a lot of people look for. And when you find it, it's terrific. And believe me, our marriage—and my wife—are terrific. ♡

Terrific marriages, terrific memories and terrific meals. You can find them in Hollywood, Houston or in Hoosick Falls. You can find them anywhere the stars shine—anywhere *your* "star" shines.

Singles—
Say So Long to Solo

What have *all* the great lovers in this book had in common? Simple. They all had partners. And, what do millions of potential great lovers out there have in common? Simple again. They all *don't* have partners.

Is it just me, or does it seem that something is seriously wrong down at Romance Central? It sure looks like the singles' switchboard is suffering from misplaced calls, bad connections and, perish the thought, all around lack of service. Any service.

It makes you wonder: "How in the heck do people find romance, anyway?" Good question. And you're about to read some very good answers from some of America's greatest lovers. Each answer is simple and direct. And each answer comes with the following Mr. Romance Guarantee: "Try it. We know it worked at least once."

But before we hear from America's most successful singles, let me set the record straight. There is no one strategy guaranteed to bag you a partner. In fact, according to the single's survey I run regularly in my newspaper column, the only consistent answer to finding a partner is that there is no consistent answer. People meet their lovers at work, at school, in phone booths, at baseball games, in the emergency room, at weddings, at funerals, in bookstores and just about anywhere anyone is.

I'm not going to waste your time by telling you to spend your life sweating at a health club to find Mr. or Ms. Ripe For The Taking. I'm going share two secrets:

1) Your chances of finding a partner increase dramatically if you believe you can find one.

Far too many singles, especially single older women, are convinced that there is no one out there for them. They quote surveys that say "single women over 40 have a better chance of getting killed by a terrorist than they do of finding a husband."

These singles would be better off listening to the 56-year-old woman who heard the same statistic and wrote in to say, "Well, I guess I'd better be on the constant lookout for terrorists."

I know it's tough to believe you can find a partner when your hopes just keep getting slammed in the brick wall of romance. But that's what this chapter is all about. Each of these singles found romance, and if they can do it, so can you.

2) Once you've spotted Mr. or Ms. Ripe For The Taking, you can make him or her yours.

You don't need a pair of Velcro panties. You just need to be open, reasonably honest and romantic. I've included a few stories of exactly how some singles snared their partners, and frankly, I think you'll be amused and amazed at what they did.

But let's start by answering that most important of all singles' questions: "Where in the world do you find a partner?" The first sensational solution comes from Linda Jo, who wrote:

SUPERMARKET SHOPPING IS A SAFEWAY TO FIND LOVE
by Linda Jo Morrison

Is the check-out line at Safeway romantic? Most people would not expect to find a meaningful relationship there, but it happened to me. Three people ahead of me stood a very distinguished looking man—neatly dressed, his beard trimmed with care. I found myself staring at him.

He turned and glanced around and then . . . our eyes met. I felt very awkward getting caught staring. I kept repeating to myself, "I am not a pick-up, I am not a pick-up." My eyes would not listen. I kept on staring.

Oops, he fumbled the money he was handing to the cashier (I also had an effect on him). But then, he picked up his bag and was leaving—oh, I wanted to meet him, but how? I couldn't just leave my groceries

123

and run after him, although it had crossed my mind. So I stayed and justified my disappointment by saying, "He *must* be married." I paid for my groceries and left.

It only happens in the movies, I thought. Outside I noticed the back of a familiar rust-colored coat standing and looking out into the parking lot. No, it couldn't be him. He waited for me? (It *was*.) While I didn't have to pass him to get into my car, I didn't want to blow a chance of meeting him. Being the cautious person that I am, I walked right behind him, hoping he would turn around and see me. He didn't and walked to his pickup. I went to my car.

Soon, a blue truck pulled up to my car—it was him. We exchanged names and he asked me if I'd like to go for a drink. So much for the cautious lady. I told him I'd meet him there. And then—at the restaurant—I sat and talked to this stranger for *three* hours. We stared at each other a lot and it all began.

New Year's Eve was the first time he said he loved me. No one else seemed to be at the party—just Frank and I. The next day at work I received a long-stemmed rose and a love note. We are now so close as friends, as lovers. Five months have passed and now we plan to marry. Romance is alive, bells do ring, you do feel dizzy. If you're single, remember my story—he or she might only be an arm's length away, even at Safeway. ♡

Kind of makes you want to run right down and park it by the passion fruit, doesn't it? Well, go ahead. We know it worked at least once.

But, if you're not a great fan of walking down those aisles for romance, how about a more traditional approach? How about the kind of fairy-tale love that can only be found in:

CINDERELLA'S SIZE-11 SLIPPER
by Lori Head

First, because it is important to the story, let me describe my Dave to you. He is 6'3" tall, weighing about 210 lbs. He is a former heavy equipment operator for an oil company on the Arctic Ocean in Alaska. He is very rugged and strong, yet gentle and loving. I met him when he came to my city to attend medical school.

We met at a start-of-school social. At a mixer function, all the women were asked to remove one of their shoes and throw it into a pile in the middle of the floor, and all the men were to take a shoe from the pile and find the proper owner. Dave (now my husband) picked a shoe for which he had no idea who the owner was, and began looking for her. It was then that he saw me. He quickly and quietly returned the shoe he was carrying to the pile and found the one that matched the one he had seen me wearing. (The fact that I wear a size 11 shoe probably helped.) We danced together most of the evening. He was wonderful. Kind of shy, yet confident.

Dave called me two days later to ask me out, but since I was involved with someone else, I told him I would not be able to go out with him. He seemed crushed, I felt terrible, and I assumed that it was over—little did I know. Dave decided that I needed time to get to know him. So . . . he looked up my schedule at school (resourceful) and found out that I was taking, of all classes, "Preparation for Marriage." To say I was shocked to see Dave in class would be a gross understatement.

You guessed it. I quickly fell for him, and every date with Dave seemed like something right out of the story books. And now our marriage does, too. ♡

Yes, single-and-still-shopping reader, those are unbelievable stories. But they're true. And your story may be just as incredible. Remember that *your chances of finding a partner increase dramatically if you believe you can find one.*

Barbara believed that she could. She took pen and paper in hand and put her faith in (drumroll) the classified ads. OK, OK, Barbara understands that you think only the truly desperate would advertise for a partner. But she would say that you're wrong. Good people advertise in the classifieds. And more important, those good people have found good partners that way. Here's Barbara's story:

I FOUND PASSION IN THE PERSONALS
by Barbara McWilliams

I'd like to comment on classified ads—they *work*. Some may think, "What kind of nerd would place or answer an ad—if they are half-way presentable they should be able to find dates without resorting to that." I tried it at the urging of my girlfriend in Texas who has been happily married for five years to a very handsome, very successful man she met through an ad. They are on a European tour right now.

I found it to be an exciting, fun experience and I was very gratified with the quality of those who wrote to me. From one ad (run for eight weeks) I received more than 50 replies and met most of them. They ranged from a handsome 33-year-old Air Force captain to a 65-year-old multi-millionaire, who was very fascinating and a very sweet person.

All were very nice looking and very successful—in alphabetical order: architect, artist, contractor, dentist, engineers, karate instructor, psychologist, realtor, stock broker, radio broadcaster, and TV personality. Each was very special in his own way, witty and fun to be with, so I had a tough time deciding. Then I received a reply from Roy. He is a gorgeous man inside and out. Roy has all the qualities I was seeking in a mate. He believes in fidelity and a lifelong commitment. He is very happy in his career as an engineer. He wasn't seeking a sex partner or "fun date." He hoped for a mate he could love and respect, just as I was. He's asked me to marry him and I'm so thankful I took the chance and placed the ad. Tell your readers—Dreams *do* come true. ♡

OK readers, listen up: Your classified dreams *do* come

true. Just be safe (don't give out your street address) and be selective (my readers say that about one in ten respondents will be "attractive"). And, dare we forget, be positive. You never know where love may strike. For example, you might even find:

LOVE ON A DOORMAT
by Marla Connor

I met the man of my dreams on my front lawn on a sunny day while I was out enjoying the warmth and studying. He was walking by and decided to introduce himself to me and to my amazement—and good fortune—we struck up an immediate friendship.

It was love at first sight in the classic sense. But what really won me was his spontaneity and wonderful sense of humor. He lay down in front of my door and asked if he could be my doormat. Then he found his way into my apartment and my life by asking to use the bathroom. He then suggested we go out for pizza but decided to order one and have it brought to his house.

After dinner, he served me ice cream with chocolate sauce (a ploy he admits using to melt my heart). But it wasn't until he stood on his hands for me and showed me his recording studio in his bathroom that I was hooked. That was our first date and I've been laughing and loving ever since. ♡

Unbelievable? Not really. You've heard that most

accidents occur within a few blocks of home? Well, most romance happens within a few feet of your face. Sometimes, in fact, you find new happiness in a very, very familiar place. One divorced woman did. Much to her amazement, she found that a past love still held:

More Than a Colonel of Truth
by Jo Drosselmeyer

My hubby is neither blazing nor boring all the time; he is such a conglomeration of both and so very un-predictable, one must be ready for anything.

After meeting him in the early 50's and marrying him to the tune of three children and 18 years of Air Force life, I divorced him. (Due to the blazing and the boring highs and lows, as well as the fact he was gone six months out of every 12 to 18 months as a navigator-bombardier.)

For three years I earned my own way and held together a household with three teenagers in turmoil. The fates interfered when—a few years later—I began studying for my Master's degree and my ex-husband came onto the campus with our youngest son to enroll him in the university. He and our son stood there, tall, good-looking, and in good humor on a sunny day. They asked me to dinner and I accepted. By the time that dinner was over, my former husband was to become my present husband again, and we are happily resuming our blazing and boring relationship.

We all have our faults, but one learns that trying

harder doesn't always make us second best, and marriages are not necessarily made in heaven. They simply require a lot of trying on both sides, during blazing *and* boring times, to lead to contentment. ♡

"Yeah sure, Langdon," I can hear you grumbling. "You want us to believe in finding love, but so far these singles have had romance jump in their grocery cart, knock on their door and walk out of the past. What's next, over the phone?"

You got it, oh perceptive reader. Here is a story that's sure to cure your hang-ups. It's called:

JUST GIVE HIM A WARM RECEPTION-IST
by Arlene Lobdell

I had been a single mom for fourteen years before Dale came into my life but the wait has been well worth it. Dale had called one of the girls in our office several times on business. I, as the receptionist, had answered all the calls and over the course of time we had started to tease each other. He asked me if it would be OK for him to call sometime to talk with just me, and I said that it would be. We carried on long conversations for three weeks before Dale asked me out.

That first date was wonderful. And on the following day, we spent the entire time on the waterfront going through all the little shops and acting like teenagers. The next day was Mother's Day and Dale called to see if he could come over for a few minutes. When he arrived, he had one dozen roses and a box of chocolates. And the next day he called to ask me out. We had a wonderful candlelight dinner at a nice little restaurant. In only fours days this wonderful man had completely stolen my heart.

P.S. We will be married on May 10th, the first anniversary of our meeting.

Preachers are fond of saying, "You gotta' *believe.*" I say it too, but I also add that you may have to be a bit sneaky, cunning and:

MORE THAN A LITTLE DARING
by Jan Redburn

I worked as a waitress in a local nightclub and to get my heartthrob's attention, I deposited a pair of tickets to a top-notch concert at my club in his mailbox with a little note attached—"Here's two tickets on me, bring a friend. See you there. You'll know me when you see me!"

We'd flirted from afar many times when he'd drive by my house in the summer, but we'd never met. I thought he was gorgeous, but I was kind of shy about actually speaking to him. Leaving those tickets and note in his mailbox was the most daring thing I'd ever done and, later that night, I regretted it of course. What if he didn't remember me? What if he had a girlfriend? I thought only the worst.

Well, miracles do happen. He brought a buddy (whew, no girlfriend), we exchanged "knowing" glances (I could tell he recognized me), but now I didn't know what to say! I suddenly got shy and wished he'd never come. If not for my meddling sister, who waitressed there too, we probably never would have gotten together.

She went over to him, told him I was "the one," and when he looked over at me and broke into a huge smile, my knees weakened and a flood of relief washed over me. From that moment on we talked and laughed like old friends. And, yes, it was the beginning of a wonderful relationship. He still tells me it was the most exciting, flattering thing that ever happened to him. ♡

So far, this most exciting thing we call love has been found:
- ♥ In the supermarket.
- ♥ Under a pile of shoes.
- ♥ Through the classified ads.
- ♥ On top of the doormat.
- ♥ Out of the past.
- ♥ Over the phone.
- ♥ Even at a busy bar.

Romance is everywhere. But first you have to believe: *1) Your chances of finding a partner increase dramatically if you believe you can find one.* Believe it or not.

And when you've found a likely candidate, it's time

to have faith in: *2) Once you've spotted Mr. or Ms. Ripe For The Taking, you can make him or her yours.*

How? Well, as these letters show, if you're open, reasonably honest and romantic, it appears as though almost *any* approach can work. For example, one single man swears:

I CAUGHT MY PARTNER IN A BRIEFCASE
by Eric Kingsford

I am an incurable romantic—55, retired, single, family raised and have a zest for life when I am in love. I am in love. My partner likes hunting and fishing and all outdoors. We had dated for 10 weeks and she had never seen me in a suit or tie. One evening she said that she did not know how she got hooked on me—so I gave her 10 or 12 good reasons and then asked what kind of man she had dreamed of.

She said he would be "reasonably good-looking, graying hair, wearing a pinstripe suit, white shirt, tie and carrying a briefcase." I told her to beware of guys with briefcases because most of them only had a cheese sandwich in them, and to stick with me and my blue jeans and she would eat ham every day.

The next night when I knocked on her door, I was wearing a blue pinstripe suit, white shirt, tie, carrying a briefcase that contained a cheese sandwich and I had sprinkled my hair with talcum powder. When she opened the door I asked her if she would like to buy some life insurance.

At first glance, she did not recognize me. When she did, she walked into the living room, sat on the sofa and pounded the pillow saying that if there was a cheese sandwich in the briefcase, she would hit me—but she didn't. In fact, she appreciated my efforts and we enjoyed one of the most romantic evenings ever. ♡

If you're interested in a decidedly more outrageous way to win the heart of your partner, you can always do what Gary Skay did. He bombarded his intended with:

ROSES, HEARTS AND A BILLBOARD
by Marilyn Mosio

I had heard people talk about the feeling you get when you fall in love. I thought they were making it up or exaggerating. Until I met Gary Skay. From Gary I've received hundreds of cards, letters and notes telling me how much he loves me. I stopped counting after I received 70 dozen roses and who knows how many I've received since then.

Gary has put numerous ads in the paper for me. There was one morning I woke up and to my surprise, in the entire yard was a gigantic heart with "I Love You" in the middle.

There were times when I would open the refrigerator and Gary had left a little love note—also, under my pillow, in the washer, in the microwave, and once he even left a note suspended from the ceiling by a string so when I woke up I would hit my head on it. What a way to wake up.

It's nothing for Gary to stand up in a booth in a restaurant and yell "I love you" and finish it off with a kiss. Some people look at him and think he's crazy, and maybe he is, but I know I wouldn't have him any other way.

I could go on and on, but the most unique way Gary has expressed his feelings has to be when he rented a billboard and painted it himself. The letters were four feet high and read: "Marilyn, I love you, Forever, Gary." What a guy. ♡

Pretty wild and crazy, no? Well you ain't heard nothin' yet. Just for the heck of it, I'd like you to read a story that details the one approach you probably shouldn't use on your intended. Though it apparently worked for these people, I don't recommend it as a way to win a lover:

I TOOK MY MAN ON A STRIP
by Yvonne White

To make a long story short, I was to be married in August, but one morning, two months before the wedding, my fiancé went to work and I haven't seen him since. Well, two months passed and I decided to throw myself a birthday party (on the day I was to be married). Along with the other guests, I invited a guy from my past who at one time was in love with me. It was at this party that I admitted to myself just how much this guy loved me.

It wasn't easy to apologize to him, plus he wouldn't let me. So I went to where he worked, where he was in a meeting in a conference room, and burst in. I had a fur coat on and said, "If this doesn't convince you, nothing will," so I turned the tape player on and went into my act. I started to slowly strip my gloves, my shoes and my stockings. He and his co-workers sat there amazed. Thank goodness, before I could finish he took me out of the room and into his office. Later that night he asked me if I would have stripped completely. I told him, "Love knows no shame, but I was hoping not to." Now, five months later, we're working on a very intimate relationship. ♡

Love knows no shame. But it does know major embarrassment. And, strangely enough, sometimes a little embarrassment is just what the romance doctor orders. In our last story of how singles have captivated their partners, we examine the case of one man and see that:

HE NIBBLED HIS WAY TO HER HEART
by Marie Higgenbottom

The moral of the story is: "The man who swallows the earring gets the girl." Dan was nibbling on my daughter Sharon's ear and he swallowed her pierced earring. He called his doctor and he sent him to the emergency room. Word spread through the hospital and soon Dan had doctors, nurses and even janitors coming in to see what he looked like. He was x-rayed and, sure enough, the earring showed up big as you please. He was hospitalized, but before he went into surgery, they were able to flush the earring from his body. While the earring was never recovered, Dan captured my daughter's heart. ♡

OK, so you didn't get a handy-dandy plan that is guaranteed to find you the perfect partner in 10 days or your money back. And you surely didn't discover the street address of where America's single men and women are hiding.

Instead what you may have learned is that it *is* possible for you to find a partner, and it *is* possible for you to capture his or her heart. These single lovers have done it. And if they could, they'd take you by the hand, sit you down and say, "You can do it too!"

Everybody Loves a Passionate Proposition

There is no sentence in the English language that holds more meaning—or stress—than "Will you marry me?" Actually translated, those four words ask:

♥ "Will you love me forever?"

♥ "Will you be my friend always?"

♥ "Will you promise not to laugh when I trip while slipping off my undies?"

A proposal of marriage is just about the most memorable moment in the lives of America's greatest lovers. And, as you've no doubt guessed, these lovers have some extraordinary, and extraordinarily surprising, stories for you. So if you are preparing to propose, get ready for some great ideas. And, if you are just here for the ride, get ready for a fun-filled trip.

139

Betsy Ann, for example, has a high-flying tale of love that can only be described as death-defying. It's called:

I'M PLANE CRAZY OVER YOU
by Betsy Ann Carlson

I would like to share with you the way my husband proposed to me. At the time that we were dating, he owned a small plane. One day he asked me to go flying with him. We had been in the air for just a short time, when he put the plane in a stall. As we zoomed to the ground—he proposed. What could I say? I guess that I still would have said yes even if we had been on the ground since we will be celebrating our 25th anniversary this year. ♡

Also having no fear of flying is a very lucky woman who experienced:

A FIRST-CLASS PROPOSAL
by Sarah Slack

Harry and I had been dating for three weeks, when one night he invited me to his home for dinner. After a candlelit meal, he placed two airplane tickets in my hand and said, "We are going to Hawaii." Not only did he make reservations to go to Hawaii, he also planned a day in Disneyland in California. While in the Magic Kingdom, he told me to go shopping for a while because he had something to do.

Back on the airplane, I was amazed to learn that Harry had booked us in first class. I took a nap on the plane and suddenly Harry woke me up. In front of me on a tray were two crystal glasses engraved with our names and the date (so that's what he did in Disneyland). The glasses were filled with champagne, along with a dish filled with orchid petals. Harry asked me to look on the bottom of the dish.

As I was going through the colorful petals, I found a big, beautiful diamond mounted on a gold band. Harry looked at me and asked, "Will you marry me?" I felt so special, surprised and anxious. Of course I said, "Yes." The entire first class, who knew all about this, applauded along with the stewardesses. ♡

And if you think that proposal rates applause, listen to what happened in this story entitled:

THE SUN NEVER SETS ON OUR LOVE
by Arlene Strauss

Aside from the little niceties my husband Gary does for me on a day-to-day basis (e.g., putting gas in my car, cooking dinner after three months of fast food, ironing a uniform for me when I'm too tired to get up on time), I will always feel that his method of proposing to me has to be the most romantic I've heard of. You see, my husband is an avid airplane pilot. He does it purely for pleasure, but it is not an interest I share.

One cool, clear evening in November, he convinced

me to take a short 15-minute plane ride to a local airport to pick up a friend. We arrived, but the friend wasn't there. As we were flying back to our original airport, Gary pulled out an old brown envelope, told me he loved me and asked me to marry him. All this against a fabulous sunset of oranges and purple and flying over Lake Erie.

Initially I thought he was teasing until I realized the envelope contained a sparkling diamond ring. This wonderful man had arranged the whole scenario so that our engagement would be special and memorable. He will always have my vote as the World's Most Romantic Man. He is an all-around nice guy who is always thinking of the other person before himself. Thanks for listening. ♡

You're welcome, Arlene. And we'll keep listening because Robert Sparkman is about to tell us the ear-catching story of "Mr. Gunz":

BRINGING OUT THE BIG GUNZ
by Robert Sparkman

It all started with my sweetheart and I strolling hand-in-hand along the shore in Texas. Just then a plane pulling a banner with the sentimental words, "Wittle Wisa Junkin Will You Marry Me?" glided along the shoreline for us and everyone else to boldly see.

The overwhelming expression on my girlfriend's face

will be one that I will remember forever. She jumped into my arms and proceeded to give me the most delectable tender-loving kiss as we passionately embraced. Just then her soft, sexy voice had found its way into my heart—for Lisa said, "Yes."

A highly cooperative and admirably accommodating gentleman I had employed approached us prominently attired in bright red suspenders, an enormous red polka dot bow tie and a large black top hat. "Mr. Gunz" then handed Lisa a box of the loveliest dozen long-stemmed red roses either one of us had ever seen. She just looked at me and said, "You're so crazy, Robert." And I said, "You're so right, I am crazy. Crazy about you."

Mr. Gunz arrived a second time carrying a strikingly beautiful champagne balloon bouquet along with two very elegant crystal champagne glasses engraved with Lisa's name on one and mine on the other. Attached to a 1976 bottle of Dom Perignon were four metallic balloons each portraying a different romantic epigram.

People around us were now responding to the growing excitement of it all. Quite a large number began to congregate around us on the beach. Meanwhile, the plane was still gracefully pulling the banner up and down the shoreline as we opened the champagne and vowed a life together as Mr. and Mrs. Sparkman. We also toasted to having a whole bunch of little Lisas and Roberts running around. Just then the group of spectators began to clap and cheer and offer their congratulations.

In the meantime, Mr. Gunz came back a third and final time holding a solid brass platter engraved with the words, "Just as the sun starts a new day, so our love will begin a new life." Placed upon the platter was a diamond ring. Tears began to glisten in Lisa's eyes and I proceeded to give her the biggest hug and kiss that I could muster. ♡

And you thought people only got sunburned on the beach. Well, they obviously do much more, especially when they jump off the sand and head for the open sea. You see, as Cheryl discovered:

OUR LOVE IS IN THE SAME BOAT
by Cheryl Richardson

When my then-boyfriend and I bought our coveted 25-foot sailboat, we had a long and very serious talk about money. Though we had been talking about getting married, he explained that, because we bought the boat, he would be financially strapped for quite a while and we would have to postpone any talk of marriage for some time. I nodded wisely, agreed that it sounded prudent and sane—and inwardly died of disappointment.

But two weeks later, when we took the boat on its maiden voyage, I resolved to make the best of it and was determined to be spunky and cheerful. When we anchored off a green and mostly deserted island for dinner,

I started the barbecue, he put the steaks on and then suggested a glass of champagne so we could properly christen our new investment. He handed out two glasses of bubbly topped with strawberries and after a while, he raised his glass to mine and quickly said, "To us." I looked into those eyes and realized how lucky I really was—married or not. I lowered my eyes to drink and, underneath the strawberry, resting gently on the bottom of the glass, lay a new and shining diamond ring. ♡

While Cheryl found her ring at the bottom of a glass, Jill was slipped hers at the bottom of a pool. Her chlorinated story of passion is entitled:

WHO CAN FATHOM LOVE?
by Jill Dominic

My husband and I had a bubbling engagement. He was a lifeguard at the time and promised to teach me to scuba dive. It was the last day of summer and he finally asked me to go for my first lesson. While I was under water trying to stay calm, a red wire appeared before my mask with an engagement ring on it. The water magnified it and I wasn't sure if it was the real thing or a bad joke. Later, everyone asked him what my reply to his proposal was and he answered, "Blup, blup." ♡

"Blup, blup." Certainly words you and I can live by. Kind of like the words, "Yes, yes, YES!" These belong to the remarkable Bonnie, who found:

LOVE ON A ROADSIDE TABLE
by Bonnie Waterman

The World's Greatest Lover and romantic has to be my husband, Art Waterman. He brings me roses unexpectedly, writes sweet love notes and calls me just to say "I love you." But the most romantic thing he ever did was when he asked me to marry him. It began with a dinner invitation, which he hand-delivered. The invitation did not say where dinner was to be, but stated that semi-formal attire was required.

On that night when he picked me up, he was wearing a sharp three-piece suit that I had not seen before. On the way to the "restaurant" he said, "You know that restaurant on so and so street? Well, we're not going there." By this time I was very curious. We were nearing a mountain pass, and I thought he might be taking me to a distant restaurant, when he pulled off the road onto a shoulder area and asked me to wait in the car. I heard a lot of noise coming from the trunk and thought he was getting out a tire. A few minutes later he opened my door and, as I got out, I was astounded by what I saw. He had set up a table, complete with tablecloth, and two chairs. On the table was a single red rose in a vase, two lighted candles, two wine glasses (which we had looked at in a store weeks earlier), cheese trays, fruit, china, napkins and silverware. He seated me, poured the wine, served the food, and we ate.

As cars drove by, the people honked, waved and cheered. Here was this set-up no more than 12 feet from the road. With a background behind us and a sunset in front of us, it was perfect. Later, he came over to my chair, knelt on one knee, took my hand in his and asked me to marry him. Of course I said, "Yes." ♡

Of course you did. But, what would you have done if your Art had *really* taken you to a restaurant? What would you have done if, like Bess, you were served:

A PLATEFUL OF FOREVER
by Bess Townsend

We had been going together for several months, when one night Bruce asked me to dinner "right" then. He picked me up and claimed he got me a special present but forgot it at home.

We went to a very small family-run restaurant, and the family for one night became "servants" to an un-suspecting princess. They did everything possible to make our evening perfect; they even put a special centerpiece on our table alone. Bruce did most of the talking about the silverware, glasses and blue trim around the plain white plates. I didn't understand his fascination with the table setting.

Then my dinner came. Fish on a bed of lettuce. Mostly I picked at it, moving it about with my fork. When I noticed black markings on my plate, I quickly moved my food aside and read, "Bess, let us join together and become one. Will you marry me? Bruce." Bruce had had a special plate made with his proposal written on it. He wanted me to remember that night forever. I was absolutely stunned. He finally said, "Well, yes or no?" I said, "Yes, I guess so," and then the owner's wife came and asked if she could clean the plate personally. She walked away with it showing other customers enthusiastically, as if she were the one just proposed to. ♡

A plateful of romance. A lifetime of love "forever." No doubt about it—it's a serious commitment. And it's the kind of commitment one uptight man had in mind when he dropped to his knees and uttered the immortal words:

WAIANAPANAPA WITH ME, WON'T YOU?
by Mary Ann Farnsworth

My love and my husband of a year-and-a-half is the most romantic man I have ever known and his brand of romance truly blazes like so many sunsets we have enjoyed together since we met two years ago.

We met at my apartment complex beside the pool on a sunny summer day (we still celebrate that day as one of our "anniversaries" along with our engagement and wedding dates). I spoke the first words as Joel climbed out of the water after a vigorous swim. Instantly, I was attracted to his warm personality. We started talking and soon discovered that we had a mutual interest in China—Joel had traveled there extensively on business—he's an importer—and I was planning a holiday there with my mother that fall. That coincidence led to Joel asking me out for a date the following evening—I accepted—and from that first dinner on we saw each other practically every day. We were falling in love very quickly.

I would come home from work (I travel in my job, too) to find notes and surprises at my doorstep. One day a couple of months after we met I came home to find a huge, six-foot-long rolled package on my living room floor. It was an incredible hand-woven silk carpet from China.

After three months of knowing each other, Joel asked me if I wanted to vacation with him in Maui, Hawaii. I accepted his invitation and we spent some wonderful days touring the island, enjoying the sun and the surf, before journeying out to the isolated town of Hana. After arriving there and checking into our gorgeous inn (the Heavenly Hana), we went to a place a few miles away called Waianapanapa Park. There we hiked along black sand beaches and lava cliffs overlooking the crashing and wild Pacific Ocean 200 feet below us. We reached the famed "blowhole" beside the park, at which point Joel asked if we could rest for a moment.

Then, he picked up his backpack and spoke of our growing love for each other. He pulled out a small

embroidered pillow which he strapped to his knee before kneeling on the lava rocks. Joel held in his hand a
small, silk box that he then opened. Out came the most
beautiful diamond ring I've ever seen, which he placed
on my finger as he asked me to marry him. I thought this
only happened in the movies, but no, it was happening
to me on this unforgettably beautiful day in Hana. ♥

Also unforgettable was one special moment in Betty's
life, though the setting wasn't Hawaii. It was New
Jersey. And it didn't take place on the beach. It happened behind some garbage containers. But they were
nice garbage containers. Betty's story is entitled:

A NEW JERSEY PICNIC PROPOSAL
by Betty Boynton

I am 67 years old and my husband is 72. We were
married in 1971, a second marriage for both. Let me tell
you how we got engaged.

I was afraid to say yes after a bad marriage, but after a
year of dating, and with Hank asking me several times
to marry him, I decided that this was my man. I loved to
go on picnics with him and even took a portable record
player with us to play our favorite song, "Picnic Time,"
by the McGuire Sisters.

So, one night when I was to pick him up at the train
from work, I made a hot casserole (his favorite), took
wine and goblets, a rose in a vase, the record player and

"Picnic Time." When he got off the train, he walked over to me and the car, which was parked in the back of a supermarket in New Jersey among three large garbage containers. There I was, with the music playing and the picnic things with a big smile on my face. As he got in, I said, "Let's get married!" And *that* was our engagement day. Right there among the garbage containers. ♡

Yessirree, proposals can be popped in the strangest of places. In a falling plane, near a bin of trash, or even:

ON THE DIAMOND OF LOVE
by Brian Falk

This story is true and relates to a friend of mine who was madly in love with a female and the game of baseball. Last January he picked up his girlfriend and told her they were going for a ride.

After a half-hour ride, they stopped in front of a baseball diamond. He suggested that she take a walk to the diamond. As she walked closer she noticed in the snow were the words, "Will you marry me? I love you. Mark." He then stood on home base. She ran to him and found a bottle of champagne and an engagement ring waiting for her arrival and acceptance. His judgment was correct. She soon became his wife and the biggest fan of baseball. ♡

The biggest fan of movies—old, romantic movies—

has to be Louise Dietrich. Her passion was piqued when she found herself:

SAYING "YES!" TO CARY GRANT
by Louise Dietrich

My boyfriend was an old-movie fanatic. One night we were watching an old Cary Grant movie. In the movie, Cary comes home from a trip and says to his girlfriend, "Go look in my right-hand suit pocket. I have a surprise for you." Simultaneously, my boyfriend said the same thing to me. When I, and the actress in the movie, reached into the suit pockets, we both found and opened boxes with diamond rings inside. Then both Cary Grant and my boyfriend dropped to one knee and said simply, "Will you be mine?" It was so beautiful and I was very proud that he researched his proposal so well, how could I say anything but, "Yes"? ♡

As we've seen, the idea for getting married in the first place usually comes from the man, or the woman, or both. But what happens when the proposal is put forth by the kids? According to Diana Ledbury, it can only be:

A FAMILY AFFAIR
by Diana Ledbury

Unlike Romeo and Juliet, there was a slight age difference between us, measured in a decade, not years—I, as the femme fatale, being older. Secondly, Romeo and Juliet is the story of a couple; ours is a love story of a group. A sizable group is what we became when we combined his kids with mine and this added up to six kids, a dog and a cat. The latter were the last to adjust. (The pets were in a state of shock. We had trouble explaining fast change to them.)

We courted in a group until they—the kids—concluded we two should marry and we eight combine. We eloped in a group with the oldest acting as witness. At 21, heaven knows she was old enough. One son acted as ring-bearer and he was proud. The rest of the kids were "boosters," cheering us on silently throughout the short ceremony.

They didn't stop cheering when we met good friends at Shakey's Pizza. The only protest we heard was from a couple of the younger kids, who asked how come they weren't at our first weddings.

Today the "yadults" (young adults) are 14, 16, 17, 18, 19 and 25. In our combined memory the picture of our wedding remains vivid. For we are the Ledbury-Lall family. We have been, are and will be. We are real, existing beyond mere story form. Boy, do we exist beyond story form. ♡

OK then, what's the story called when the proposal is amorously offered—not by your boyfriend, or girl-friend, or family—but by your husband? It can only be:

HAPPINESS IS A HEARTFELT HUBBY
by Mrs. Daphne Wiatrowski

My husband has put up with me freezing his sweaters on the line (I hand washed them, hung them to dry and then it began to snow), burning tuna casserole and setting off the smoke alarm, and more. Now that you have the general idea of how special he is, let me share my most romantic memory.

It was just after our son was born. As couples with a newborn know, mommies and daddies have little time together. My husband offered to put the little guy down for the evening and told me to soak in a hot tub with the door closed. When I finished and opened the door, I found blankets, pillows, and candles flickering in the living room. Music was softly playing on the radio and I received a massage with hot towels and baby oil.

Under one of the pillows, I found a small ring box. Inside was a beautiful diamond engagement ring (the night before our wedding, my engagement ring accidentally found its way into the garbage disposal.) Needless to say, my new ring and I intend to stay put and grow old with my best friend—my husband. ♡

A diamond ring would surprise almost any wife. But what does it take to surprise a young couple desperately in love? What does it take to make a man and woman yell:

WE DO! WE DO!
by Susan Gibson

My fiancé and I wanted to go away for a wedding and honeymoon, so we decided on Florida. In Tallahassee we took care of the license and blood test. Then, we looked for a photographer from the Yellow Pages and went to meet her and make arrangements. She suggested having the wedding outside of the local art museum. We liked the idea, so everything was decided, but not scheduled.

Before the wedding, we did some traveling and sightseeing for three days. When we returned and were walking toward the museum's outdoor gardens, a group of people was there. I thought we were interrupting someone else's wedding. Just then they all shouted "Surprise!" to us. We couldn't believe it. In three short days this fantastic lady had arranged an entire wedding for us—complete with a cake and champagne. All of her friends, family and co-workers were part of the wedding party, including bridesmaids, groomsmen, a maid of honor and a best man.

There was also a wonderful guitarist. To top it off, local reporters were there as the mayor gave us the key to the city. Then they announced that we would be staying at the Tallahassee Hilton and having dinner at a very elegant restaurant as their *guests*. Our wedding was more romantic than I ever dreamed of and all because of one special lady who cared. She gave us the memory of a lifetime. ♡

And the proposal of most anyone's lifetime was offered to Carole when her boyfriend stepped from the story books and appeared as:

MY KNIGHT IN SHINING ARMOR
by Carole Johnson

Last year on the morning of July 15th, I was working as a loan clerk at a local bank. I had an appointment with my boyfriend, Scott Johnson, for lunch at 12:00 p.m. The entire preceding week he had been telling me that I was in for a surprise, which I would receive on the 15th day of that month. He had even picked out the outfit that I was to wear on that day. I had just figured that he was going to take me somewhere special in view of my birthday which is the 27th of July.

At 10 minutes till twelve I was approached by my boss who informed me that my paycheck had been lost in the mail and was waiting for me at our other branch across the parking lot. Grabbing my arm, she stated that we should get it immediately!

When we got outside I noticed that about 200 people were standing around looking down the street. As I was catching my breath, I also noticed that many eyes were on me and many cameras were flashing. Coming down the street was a young man draped in a red velvet cape and a Roman gladiator outfit carrying a dozen red roses and a red satin pillow. Not far behind him was another man riding a beautiful white Arabian steed draped in the same red satin with gold dangles. The man on the horse was wearing armor and a red cape.

As they approached, I realized that the man on the horse was my boyfriend, Scott, and the young man on foot was his brother Jeff. When Scott dismounted from the horse, he stood before me, and taking my hand he knelt down on one knee and handed me the roses carried by his "squire." I was in such shock that I couldn't speak or move.

He proposed to me with tear-filled eyes, and when I spoke in an inaudible reply of "Yes," he took a beautiful ring from the satin pillow and placed it on my finger.

There were many people to witness this wonderful event, including the *Idaho Statesman* newspaper. Many friends and family had been informed beforehand of Scott's proposal and helped him to plan it and keep it completely from my knowledge. We now have a videotape of the entire event along with many lasting memories to cherish forever.

Scott and I are to be married on May 12th. We are both very excited and are looking forward to our new life together. ♡

Will they love each other always? Will they be best friends forever? Will they promise not to laugh? Sure these great American lovers will. They've learned that everyone loves a passionate proposition. They've discovered the courage—and the creativity— to take that first great step to a lifetime of love.

And, kind reader, if you'll allow Yours Truly to take the first step toward a lifetime of love, let me simply ask:

"Emmeline Alyce Kunde, will you marry me?"

I'll keep you posted.

Given Half a Chance, Your Romance Will Last a Lifetime

You've met a lot of America's Greatest Lovers in this book, including:

Dennis and Cheryl Shepard, who found love when their guide dogs lunged at each other;

Sally and Clayton Young, who overcame all obstacles to treasure the meaning of "forever";

P. T. Thompson, who laughed and loved on "The Night Modesty Blazed";

The Pence Family, who found their affection swimming in a bowl of Tearwater Chili;

The one and only Patrick, who gleaned the meaning of romance from the sound of his parents' shower;

Linda Carlson, who was touched by the heartfelt meaning of a hand-washed uniform;

Lorne Greene, whose memory still hears the sweet music of a strumming ukelele;

Eric Kingsford, who proved his love with a briefcase and a cheese sandwich;

And Carole Johnson, who dared to dream for her knight in shining armor.

Every one of them is a truly great lover. But the greatest lover you have met in this book is *you.* You met that great lover when you read that one story and whispered, "That reminds me of the time I . . . ." You rediscovered that great lover when you remarked, "We did it even better when . . . ." And you touched that great potential lover in you when you thought, "I wish my relationship could be like that, too."

You *are* America's Greatest Lover. You've always had the power, the knowledge and the ability to create that truly great love of your life. If anything, these stories have only given you the one small thing that you may have lacked: The hope. The hope that says, "Given half a chance, my love will last a lifetime."

And it's that hope that adds the crowning touch to the lives of our final great American lovers, the Kirby's. Their story is called:

DANCING & ROMANCING, FOREVER
by Debbie Kirby

My husband is a one-of-a-kind guy, for I know in my heart how special and rare he is. I know my husband loves me after 11 years of marriage when he still insists on doing the "Y" dance when we go dancing. This is where he folds his arms around me tightly, looks deeply and tenderly into my eyes, and barely moves his feet while wearing that boyish grin of his that says, "Why dance?"

I also received a special gift all wrapped and left on my night stand before he left for work. He works for a gypsum company and was working through the nights for a period of time. There he had made me a sculpture of himself out of gypsum rock. Under one eye was a big tear. The inscription read, "I miss you so much when I'm away."

He also gave me a silver dollar on our first date together. We were at a local night club and the waitress gave him two matching silver dollars as change. He gave one to me and vowed to always carry the match to mine. That was 14 years ago and he hasn't missed a day. The face is now completely worn from that loving silver dollar. And I know he loves me when the kids (they're ten, nine and six) say, "Aw Mom, aw Dad—not *again*. Kissie, kissie, kissie." ♡

Go ahead. Believe in your story. Believe in your romance. Then get ready to write your very own book of love.